# JANUS
# PRINCIPLE

## FOCUSING YOUR COMPANY ON SELLING TO SMALL BUSINESS

The Why, Who, What, Where, When and How of organizing the company to more effectively market to small business leaders. Based on 10+ years of advising small business leaders and corporations on creating, managing and growing enterprises.

BY
### JoAnn Mills Laing
*Chairman, Information Strategies, Inc.*

AND
### Donald Mazzella
*Chief Operating Officer, Information Strategies, Inc.*

Brick Tower Press
New York

Brick Tower Press
1230 Park Avenue
New York, New York 10128

Library of Congress cataloging-in-Publication Data
JoAnn Mills Laing and Donald Mazzella
The Janus Principle
Includes glossary and index
ISBN13: 978-1-883283-70-4

1. Laing, JoAnn Mills, —

2. Mazzella, Donald, —

Trade Paperback, Nonfiction, Business and Economics,
Small Business, Marketing

Library of Congress Control Number: 2009927657
First Edition, October 2009

# DEDICATION

This book is dedicated to the thousands of small business leaders, marketers and customers who have contributed to our knowledge base.

In surveys, personal interviews, focus groups and in many research and information venues, these men and women have opened themselves up to our probing questions and analysis.

Many marketers have also contributed to this book by providing us with data and unfettered access to their efforts.

Then, too, is the staff of Information Strategies, Inc., whose efforts have helped us reach such a valued industry postion and who coninue to do outstanding work.

# CONTENTS

# INTRODUCTION

As a market for selling products and services, American small business would outrank all but the top ten of the world's nations. For that reason, this sector is alluring to many companies eager to expand sales and improve profits. But like any market, foreign or domestic, there are mores and customs that need to be understood to be successful.

By understanding the fundamental imperatives that motivate and drive small business leaders, marketers can more effectively shape, sell and deliver their products and services. Equally as important is the need for companies marketing to this area to better organize themselves to succeed. Most do not, and as a result, leave many opportunities unfilled or short of expectations.

Therein lies the theme and purpose of this book.

After more than ten years of serving as an advisor to corporate marketers and mentor to small business leaders, we are confident that there are myths and misconceptions existing on both sides of the sales equation.

Since the turn of the century, *Information Strategies, Inc. (ISI)*, our company, has conducted more than 100 surveys for its publications and clients. These surveys of small businesses from 2-500 employees have given us insight in how they think and how they buy. We have conducted focus groups, reviewed client campaigns, and managed to assemble an audience of more than five million small and medium size business leaders. It is from these efforts and at the suggestion of some of our clients that we have distilled our experiences into this book.

Like any country, there are different segments and sub-cultures that make up "the small business market." For many marketing companies, small businesses are those with up to 100 employees and $100 million in sales. For others, this target gets down to 50 employees and just $50 million in sales. Still smaller market segments are defined as up to 20 employees and just $10 million in sales.

*At ISI, we have a different way of looking at this market. When someone refers to their enterprise as "my company", it is a small firm often referred to as small to medium-sized enterprises or SMEs. When they refer to the organization as "the company," for marketing purposes it passes into the sub-sector of a larger enterprise.* One only has to hear an organization's president to know the difference and classify the company. For this book, we like to think our suggestions and thoughts apply mainly to firms from very small (with under five employees) to companies with less than 100 employees and/or $50 million in sales.

Throughout this book we will call the target audience "small business leaders." ISI's experience, and those of other successful marketers, shows that in most cases, a small enterprise has one "leader" and many implementers. Often this is the leader/president and it is he or she that makes a majority of the buying decisions. In the case of partnerships, the most successful are those where one partner is responsible for certain functions and the other partner(s) handles the rest.

For the successful marketer, the process centers on two tasks:

➤ Marshalling the firm's resources to produce the products and services; and
➤ Identifying and selling the right decision maker.

This book is divided into six major parts –the Why, Who, What, Where, When and How of marketing to small business. In the first part, we will talk about "Why" the small business sector is so appealing; then "Who" is the target audience and the successful marketer.

We will move on to the "What" of how the two expect to sell and buy. The next parts discuss the "Where" and "When" they purchase. We devote the final section to the "How" of success, providing tools strategies and tactics.

Throughout this book we will also discuss the *Janus Principle*. *
Essentially, it is the methodology by which the successful marketer can better manage the process of marshaling the seller's resources to provide the product/service that will profitably appeal to the small business leader.

---

*Janus is the Roman god of gates and doors, beginnings and endings, and hence represented with a double-face head, each looking in opposite directions.

# THE JANUS PRINCIPLE

There are really two "whos" in any marketing situation – the seller and the buyer.

In ancient times and over every Roman doorway was a motif showing the two-headed god Janus. He was shown looking out and looking in. A marketer is like that Janus – looking outward to sell and inward to marshalling the company's resources to produce the product or service. Since we have grown accustomed to labeling everything and everyone, we have encapsulated this process into the *Janus Principle*. The concept grew out of our work with large corporations, both as senior executives, consultants and observers.

The *Janus Principle* is in reality a process that centers on understanding the marketplace and the organization's own internal prejudices. In short, the *Janus Principle* enables the marketer to proceed on the basis of not what the organization wants or expects but rather what can be done to meet the marketplace's needs. Once this internal, external dichotomy is understood, each marketer creates a methodology that enables his or her company to successfully produce and market products/services that others will buy.

Mastering the *Janus Principle* helps marketers to successfully bridge the gap between their company and the targeted marketplace.

## Bridging The Gap

More specifically, we focus on the *Janus Principle* to help explain how to successfully sell to leaders. In our experience, there is a significant distortion between large corporations and their expectations and small business enterprises and their approach to purchasing goods and services.

To give this concept a different perspective, let's look at it this way. *Whereas large corporations were created to control the business functions, small firms are set-up to get things done.* By their sheer size, large corporations must focus on managing their resources. Small business leaders earn profits by getting things done quicker, with less time-to-market, and more conveniently.

While big corporations set the tone and pace of America's economy, it is small business managers who provide the lubricant that keeps it running.

From the corner dry cleaner to the Internet service provider through to the local sign maker, small business personnel service big corporations and the public-at-large. How they accomplish these tasks and keep their firms profitable is, in many ways, different from their bigger brethren. This dichotomy also extends to the process of selling products and services to these differing audiences.

In a large corporation, the purchasing process moves through consensus and adaptation. Within a small firm, purchasing is a matter of deciding between a set of finite variables, usually time and money.

In approaching small business to sell a product and service, the successful marketer learns to put aside some preconceived notions and recognize that there are differences that must be bridged and adaptations made.

The marketing leaders in many larger organizations have never experienced the small business environment. They have never gone to the post office at 4:55 pm to get a package out. They never met payroll at 11:30 pm or filled in at the shipping station. For the large corporate manager, success is measured by building consensus. The small business leader measures success by getting tasks done.

The big corporate manager and the small business manager exist in different cultures. Bridging that cultural divide and demonstrating that the *Janus Principle* needs to be kept in mind at all times is one of the key elements of this book.

## Smaller Enterprise Participants

The *Janus Principle* is also important for smaller enterprises seeking to sell to other small businesses.

Many entrepreneurial companies seeking to sell to other smaller enterprises fail to grasp a concurrent reality. Small business leaders do not rush out to buy new, unproven products or services. The entrepreneur with a new way of delivering a product or service knows his or her product intimately. It is what one pundit described as "The Curse of Knowledge." They know it is good and can save money. In contrast, the small business leader who is a target for that product or service often knows little or nothing about the offering or the company behind it.

There used to be an ad for McGraw-Hill trade publications that featured an older man looking into the camera and saying: "I don't know your company. I don't know you. And I don't know your product. Now – Sell me!" That is the dilemma facing a smaller entrant into the small business sector.

What both the large corporation and the smaller sales enterprise face in common is a healthy dose of buyer wariness, which permeates most small business leaders. And, as it will be shown in these pages, there are solid reasons for thinking so.

The final question is: "Why should I read this book?" That's a question best answered in the following way:

Because you will learn how to better market to one of the largest audiences on earth – the American small business leader.

For the past decade, our staff and I have been helping large corporations market to small business leaders while helping this audience better manage their enterprises.

On the following pages we will talk about more specific, successful ways of selling to small business leaders. But, first let's look at some of the key myths in marketing to small businesses.

## Small Business Myths

In our studies and surveys, we have found that marketers have very distinct ideas on what constitute the drivers within the small business marketplace. These concepts often fuel the direction and spend of marketing efforts for many large corporations and smaller enterprises.

The successful marketers to small business, and there are many, often take these assumptions and put them on their heads. It is from these marketers and our own experiences that form the basis of our thoughts and suggestions. Herewith is our list of the most commonly reported myths of small business marketing.

→ Myth 1: Small business leaders are risk takers.
→ Myth 2: Because you're big/technology leader means small businesses will buy your product/service.
→ Myth 3: Small business leaders make buying decisions during the day.
→ Myth 4: Because we're a big brand you should buy our products.
→ Myth 5: "What's good for General Motors is good for small businesses."
→ Myth 6: Small business leaders spend money when they see some thing to help them.
→ Myth 7: The bigger the endorser, the more potent the message.
→ Myth 8: Successful small business marketing focuses on a national landscape.
→ Myth 9: Small business leaders will adapt their company to the product/service offering.
→ Myth 10: National business publications are the key to selling small business leaders.
→ Myth 11: Pricing is not as important as other factors in the buying decision.
→ Myth 12: Credit cards fuel small business growth and buy decisions.
→ Myth 13: Costco and Wal-Mart do not affect the buy decision.
→ Myth 14: Small businesses can be sold over the phone and through the mail.
→ Myth 15: Call centers can sell products/services as well as salespeople.
→ Myth 16: A one-size-fits-all response kit can be effective.

# THE WHY

There are several "whys" inherent in this book.

The first is: "Why this book?"

Over the past years that we have been serving the small business market, our staff and we have noticed several things.

First and foremost is that small businesses represent one of the country's largest economic sectors, and, coupled with their buying power as professional managers and consumers, it is a market not to be ignored.

Second, we have noticed the significant differences between the people selling to the small business marketplace and their audiences. This dichotomy has resulted in many forays being less successful than they could have been.

Third, we can help save millions of dollars that would be otherwise wasted in these efforts if companies spent time organizing themselves to reflect the markets they are serving, i.e. focus on getting things done in the same way their target audience conducts business rather than simply gaining internal consensus.

If the dollars saved by these efforts were used to reduce the delivery costs of products/services, then the economy as a whole would benefit. We believe this book is especially timely in an era of financial distress, uncertain business conditions and high unemployment.

Finally, the small business leader deserves more respect than he or she often gets from the individuals that market to them.

## Market Size

As we said at the beginning of this book, the small business marketplace is larger than almost every country in the world. At the same time, it is a diverse culture with many different components.

Identifying the right marketing mix – product, price, promotion, and place – requires considerable time and effort. Moreover, the research needed make such an identification is often time consuming, narrow in scope and difficult to analyze. Our own experience, over 10+ years, also shows that it is dynamic in its trends and at the same time static in its features.

While it is true that only one of five small businesses survives more than five years, once past that point, statistics consistently show they are relatively stable.

To give an example, of our list of 5+ million small business managers, more than 81% have been with us for more than three years. More than 50% are in our database at the same location and with the same email for more than seven years.

Contrast this with the average corporate manager's position tenure of about 18 months.

Every year, we update our business addresses and for four years running, address changes averaged less than 3% versus a normal rate of 19% for the population as a whole.

Here are some figures from the *National Federation of Independent Businesses* to consider:

- Salaries and benefits average 55% in small businesses versus 42% in larger corporations.
- In terms of U.S. Gross National Product, small businesses represent 66% of all goods and services.
- Small businesses created 97% of all new jobs since 1997.
- On average, the five million companies in our database have at least 1.2 computers per employee.
- Small businesses have one telephone per employee versus 1.3 telephones per employees in the Fortune 1000 corporations.

➺ Despite this difference per employee, more than half of all business phones in the U.S. are in small firms.

As these examples show, small businesses represent a sizeable marketplace that is well worth selling into. But doing so often requires the selling company to make radical changes in the way its staff looks at this marketplace.

## Contrasting Staffing

Let's take a look at the average manager from a large corporation and then from smaller enterprises that are charged with selling to this marketplace.

The average position tenure of a manager in large corporations is 18 months. This stint covers one and half sales cycles in most instances. This manager is often rotated into the position as part of a career path leading to senior management.

In our talks and assignments with these managers, we have observed a strong dichotomy in several areas with their target audience. These comments reflect our observations and are not meant to be negative. They are, however, meant to reflect the differences in the two groups and hence the necessity for adopting the *Janus Principle* to the marketing entity.

Many managers have never had to meet a payroll. Few have true budget responsibilities and the company is not at risk should the offering(s) fail to be delivered or succeed.

For smaller enterprises, there are usually younger staffs in place to carry out the execution of the firm's battle plan. We have come to understand that in the IT and Internet area particularly, employees are often working for entrepreneurs who themselves do not have the breadth of experience or skills needed to effectively market to small business leaders.

As a result, the marketing often reflects the mores of the organization, rather than the needs of the audience.

## Efficient Marketing

Houston economist Dr. Kenneth E. Lehrer estimates that if industries selling to small business leaders would improve their efficiencies by just 1%, they would save almost $500 million in costs. He based this on the overall direct marketplace cost of $50 billion in goods and services expended each year by small businesses.

One way companies can reduce their costs is to be more efficient in their marketing. In later chapters, we identify resources that can be more effectively utilized in the marketing process.

Reduced costs mean a more profitable bottom line or alternatively lower prices for goods and services. Lehrer points out in his studies that as fuel costs rose in the early 1970s American companies found ways of improving the yield from energy sources through more efficient motors, recovery processes and distribution methods.

*UPS* is saving millions of dollars each year simply by more efficiently routing its drivers. One way is to plan routes that required only right hand turns. This simple example demonstrates that efficiencies are possible.

In terms of marketing, one simple example is to clean mailing lists to avoid duplication and sending to moved or defunct operations.

List managers tell us that many companies have abandoned this exercise as the managers in position to authorize them are in place for shorter periods of time. But sending direct mail to employees no longer at an establishment is often seen as an indication that they, the small business leaders and their companies, are not worth the bother of updating lists.

Besides being counterproductive, the practice is wasteful and adds to overall marketing costs.

We discuss more easily implemented efficiencies later on.

## Viewing the Small Business Leader

Perhaps the most glaring omission on the part of company managers is their view of small business leaders.

Particularly in large corporations, there seems to be an over-whelming attitude that somehow small business leaders are less intelligent than their corporate counterparts. At the same time, these managers, often beset by internal politics and unable to control their own destinies, speak wishfully of "running their own show."

For many, in this age of corporate downsizing, the wish becomes a reality. We have observed many managers in transition to their own companies. Examples of this difficult transition are legion. The funniest was when one ex-CFO of a multi-billion dollar company called us and asked how he got stamps.

Most small business leaders work hard at managing their firms. The successful ones put in 24/7 days. Corporate managers by contrast are rarely at their jobs for more than 50 hours a week, many much less.

One manager could not understand how anyone could work the hours his clients said they did. This view is not pointed at every manager but it is detailed to demonstrate how critically important it is for the company to fully understand its audience.

To be sure, there are corporations with great marketing acumen when it comes to small business leaders. It is from them that we learn many of the lessons that have made us significant players in the small business space.

This book and the *Janus Principle* it espouses are a reflection of their activities as much as ours.

## The Elephant and The Blind Men

In the tale of the elephant and the blind men, each feels the animal from a different perspective (trunk, leg, tail) and describes the whole subject in a different way. So do "experts" talk about small business leaders. Each viewer has a different perspective.

Defining a whole sub-culture into a single matrix is almost impossible. What can be done is provide an outline of the sometimes contradictory traits of successful small business leaders. While they come in many shapes, sizes background, personalities and professional training, they do have some things in common:

➤ Stick-to-itness
➤ Willingness to work hard
➤ Drive to succeed
➤ Focus on their business
➤ Willingness to take a calculated risk
➤ Fiscal restraint
➤ Modicum of luck

Knowing more about these individuals who are in a position to purchase goods and services is key to building additional products.

# THE WHO

Like many other economic and social sectors, there are many different strata of small business. In this section, we will talk about "The Who" of small business, some myths and ways of understanding and overcoming them as marketers. More specific recommendations are addressed under "The How" section of this book.

## Who Is a Small Business Leader?

When many of the nation's largest firms look to smaller enterprises to fuel their profits, they take into account the true drivers in the purchasing process. At the same time, they have learned to interpret the differences between how their organizations manage the purchasing process and those drivers that impel their customers.

In short, they have put the *Janus Principle* to work.

However, many more corporations and companies have not yet learned the differences. Over the past ten years, our studies have shown that small business managers have a decision-making process that differs widely from those that drive corporate managers. Understanding this process is key to successfully selling to small businesses for the large corporate marketer and the budding entrepreneur.

Small businesses consume office supplies, technology, consulting services, as well as equipment, finance and a host of other products and services they use to operate their companies. To large corporations and new entrepreneurs, they are often thought of as the "low hanging fruit" which can be easily exploited. In truth, small business leaders can be the most difficult sales targets. For the marketer, the key to success is finding this decision maker and convincing him or her to purchase the product or service being offered.

In popular folklore, small business leaders are risk takers. This perception fosters an image of the daring entrepreneur who seeks out challenges and conquers them before lunch. Often they are portrayed as the precursor of innovative ideas and concepts that become new divisions of larger corporations. While it is true that for many reasons, small business leaders tend to take more risks when it comes to doing something different, the reasons for doing it may not be so romantic or heroic.

Sometimes, small businesses are formed out of necessity or happenstance. Many come about because there are no alternatives open to the founders. Or, they inherit a business from a father or, increasingly in this century, from a mother, and continue the legacy. Many are simply people who want to run their own shop.

Some are people, usually women, who for one reason or another can't take or hold a full-time position. For some women it is because of family responsibilities. Often, a home-based hobby becomes a business.

Another trend we are seeing is that of women whose husbands have died or left, they often take over the business and, sometimes to their surprise, thrive along with the enterprise.

For other leaders, it is the need to be in an environment that gives them the opportunity to do other things. Interestingly, when more than 1100 corporate business managers responded to a 2008 survey on whether they had examined franchising as an alternative to their current employment, one in three (37%) were looking for an activity totally separate or different from their own work experience.

Older Americans see small business leadership as an opportunity to take a hobby and turn it into a profitable venture. Some men go into business with their wives after retiring from a corporate position. Another factor is the growth of small firms owned by immigrants and their children. Proof of their growth is seen in the billions of dollars exported yearly from Americans to other countries in the form of individual postal and bank money orders. While it is true a large percentage of these payments are from immigrant workers, studies by several money center banks reveal that small business leaders are also purchasers of these fund transfer vouchers.

Despite these realities, many marketers take as a given that small business leaders are early adopters and that the qualities that made them entrepreneurs also make them more open to new ideas, products and services. With this assumption, they proceed with the idea that if they create the product or service, the small business leader will come. The truth is that in the day-to-day management of their enterprises, small business leaders are more conservative than that.

There are also millions of small company leaders who are willing or unwilling refugees from large corporate environments. These individuals have a second set of imperatives that need to be always considered. For many, the long training in a corporate environment makes them even more risk averse than their brethren who willingly chose entrepreneurship from the beginning.

Put simply, although they have been willing to take a leap of faith by launching their company, they are "very conservative" when it comes to spending their hard-earned cash for expenditures.

In survey after survey done by our company and others, this dichotomy surfaces in a variety of ways. Small business leaders do have certain characteristics that keep them as a driving force on the road to success. For these managers, the decision process is overlaid with a strong analytical emphasis touched with a layer of doubt that needs to be addressed in the marketing process.

Successful small business ventures have several things in common – persistence, hard work, an eye-on-the-bottom line and willingness to trade effort for financial expenditure. This sort of environment breeds a potential client who thinks three times before buying something new. He or she seeks out advice, often from friends or neighbors or other small enterprise leaders. What they won't do is take the word of someone they don't know.

There are also contradictions in the small business leader. These contradictions make for a complex individual, who has conflicting imperatives that must be addressed in a successful marketing campaign. Many small business leaders take great chances to start and expand their business. For many individuals, if often means risking everything. As Bill Cosby described at an awards ceremony, "John Johnson sold his mother's furniture to start *Jet* magazine. If he had failed, he would have gone to jail." For many entrepreneurs, this approach is often the only avenue open to them. In offering products or services, marketers must keep all these realities in focus.

Successful marketers realize that in dealing with this community the rules of corporate life are often turned upside down. For large corporate managers, the decision-making process often focuses on consensus building. This focuses their efforts and takes up a significant amount of time during the business day.

For the small business leader, the decision is often made alone and with little consultation or based on advice from sources not usually identified by large corporations as influencers. Once made, the decision is acted upon and he or she goes back to the activities of managing the company's sales and marketing efforts.

Because they lead enterprises with limited resources, small business leaders have little time or the wherewithal to revisit decisions, once made. Buyers' remorse is not an emotion small business leaders can have for long.

In addition, small business leaders don't like a disruption in their business that comes from bringing in a new product. They don't want to be the "first," or the guinea pig; they want someone else to have "blazed the trail" before them.

If a reference sell is used in the marketing effort, small business leaders want "reliable" references from other small businesses that have used the products or services in the past, before they will even consider making a purchase. And they want themselves and their staff not to have to spend a lot of time trying to figure out instructions or getting bogged down, wasting valuable time on the phone trying to speak to a customer service or technical installation person.

Equally as important, small business leaders value the personal touch. They like the feeling that the supplier is talking to them directly and knows something about their enterprise. Small business leaders believe that no one knows their business better then they do. But they do appreciate when someone takes the time to try to understand what he or she is trying to accomplish.

The difference in outlook is best shown by telephone usage. Call a small business and you are more liable to get someone answering the phone. Call a large corporation or a customer service number and the opposite is true.

Put another way, the personal touch works wonders. Years ago, there was a *United Airlines* commercial about a company that lost touch with its clients. The theme could be repeated for many marketers today. They seem to have lost touch with their clients and have little desire to change that.

Small business leaders also view big corporations as competitors and threats.

For the past 25 years, smaller companies have been fighting the retail trend of "big box" stores. The local stationary store, the local hardware store, the local lumberyard are mostly an establishment of the past.

When *Home Depot* traded out experienced sales people for a less knowledgeable, albeit cheaper floor staff, it lost customers by the droves. The final straw for many smaller contractors occurred when it started contracting out services in direct competition. When this happened, overall sales suffered.

More than ten million businesses have *Pitney Bowes* equipment installed on their premises. Yet, when that company switched to electronic updating and other methods of charging its postage meters, it suffered, and continues to suffer from poor relations.

One final thought on small business leaders. They depend on the people around them for advice and guidance. The *UPS* deliveryman they see every day has more impact on the sales process than one might imagine. So too, for the local druggist, plumber, family, Internet expert and others with whom they have regular contact.

The small business leader is an elusive marketing target, but he or she is just down the street if you look hard enough

## The Personal Touch

We recently appeared on a podcast about 2.0 innovations and its impact on small business marketing.

It was evident the host had an agenda pushing the Internet as a valuable tool for small business marketers.

His justification was that the Internet spreads the marketplace for small businesses and therefore gives them more opportunity to be successful.

We could hardly disagree with this moderator but were surprised when he thought that eventually the Internet would be the prime marketing venue in the future.

There is no question that it has and will have a major impact on marketing; for marketers to small business leaders, we strongly urge them not to abandon the personal touch.

One example to think about: many small business leaders resent having to talk to Indians, Pakistanis, and Filipinos when asking for technical support or even purchase products.

There is still a bias towards American-based enterprises. On the other hand, immigrants running their own businesses do not suffer from such a bias.

# THE WHAT

While larger firms and corporations think in millions of dollars, small businesses operate in terms of hundreds of dollars. So, it makes sense that a corporate marketing department must learn how to craft products and services to fit these "smaller clients."

## Crafting Products and Services Specifically to Fit Smaller Clients

The important point to remember in all of the company's development efforts is that the small business leader wants a hassle-free product/service that will add dollars without requiring significant changes in the way the company operates. Product development should start with the ultimate audience – small businesses in mind – and be kept at the top of the list at all times.

In marketing, there are the "four Ps" – product, price, place and promotion. For our purposes we will start with "The What," which is the product.

There are many successful products that draw the attention and dollars of small business leaders. None, more so, than *Intuit*'s suite of products. But for every *Intuit*, there are hundreds of other equally good products that languish because they do not satisfy a need while reducing costs without severe dislocation.

Let's start with one very common misconception.

Most corporate executives do not recognize they cannot just "downsize" a product or service and say it is a small business offering.

The bygone comic strip *L'il Abner* featured a villain called General Bullmoose who parodied a famous statement by the head of a large auto company. To wit, "What's good for General Motors is good for the USA."

Many large corporations have offered a "watered down version" of a product to small business clients. Their argument is that this product or service works well for large corporations, why shouldn't it work as well for smaller enterprises. The plain truth is that in many situations we have seen, a product adopted from an offering used in larger corporations has many drawbacks for smaller companies.

Large corporations have the ability and resources to install and manage new concepts and offerings. In most cases, small businesses do not. *IBM* learned that in its Point-of-Sales division. It tried to adapt systems that worked in large franchise operations to industrial sectors that were essentially "mom-and-pop" operations.

Not until they stepped back and looked at the field from the clients' perspective did they come up with a profitable solution. We'll go into that example later on but for now keep this concept in mind when deciding to cut down a big company product for the small business market.

Small business leaders and executives are a smart group of people. They are good at what they do: managing and operating a small business and enjoying a profit each month. And in order to continue on that road to success, they will carefully evaluate every marketing and promotional advertisement and piece of literature that comes across their desk. Their preference is to add products/services when they can be shown to improve profits or reduce costs. They are also concerned that the product/service will not disrupt their business should it fail to live up to expectations.

High-speed Internet connections are a blessing to many businesses. However, the first group of offerings required significant investment in product and installation in order to make a company fully functional. This first onslaught failed when a major provider went bankrupt leaving many small businesses with equipment and services they couldn't use.

The second wave of DSL providers, particularly *Verizon*, learned from this fiasco and made installation and maintenance easy and almost trouble free. Still, most small business leaders refer to the debacle when talking about new IT innovations.

A product/service needs to fit the small business and not require the organization to change to accommodate the new product/service. That is a myth weighing on many marketers.

There is a current trend to sell small business leaders on the advantages of what is called 2.0 services. In addition to improved web technology and design aimed to enhance creativity, information sharing and user collaboration, it is used by some providers to bundle the power of the Internet into service modules to do everything from accounting, inventory control, sales management, and distribution. While growing in usage, this approach requires a fundamental change in the way a small business operates. In conferences and meetings, *ISI* has heard complaints that the cost of getting small business leaders to adopt these product offerings is prohibitive.

The leader of a world-class support product based on 2.0 technologies reported that of 631 leads generated by Internet marketing, he had four demonstrations and no sales. When queried further, it turned out that his product required among other things, that the business leader needed to change his company's phone number in order to truly integrate into his suite of products.

By now one should understand his problem.

No matter what type of product (or service) they are considering purchasing, small business leaders want it to be "very simple to use." They want to be able to open a box, spend two minutes or less, and be "up and ready to go." So, the easier the company makes it, the more satisfied the small business leader will become. And that can translate into "lots of repeat business."

Also, when they are very pleased with the product or service, they will share that information with their friends and associates. And in the world of small business leaders and managers, the "power of a referral" is worth its weight in gold!

The myth that says that small business leaders spend money when the product/service can help them is just that, folklore rather than reality.

For successful small business leaders, the overriding mantra is focused on conserving cash. They would rather trade "time for money." They don't mind putting out the time, but their real need is to "hold on to their cash." Although business failures due to lack of cash dipped in the early years of the 21$^{st}$ century, four out of five small businesses will fail, and the primary reason is because they "run out of money." No matter how hard they have tried to hold on to their precious cash, it seems to leave faster than it comes in, which can spell disaster for a small business leader.

They will not make snap decisions to buy the company's product or service. Instead, they will carefully dissect what the company is offering to them to see if it fits the "small business model." In other words, they want to make sure the company is marketing to *them,* the small business leader, and not to another giant corporate client.

*This approach is best summarized by the Janus Principle. Don't base your efforts on your company's view of the world but rather on that of your customers' mindset.*

Our research over the last ten years points to several recurring themes that help to prevent successful marketing to small business leaders. They include but certainly are not limited to:

**Not identifying the need or want of the product/services aimed at smaller companies and businesses.** Until corporate marketing departments get rid of the "one size fits all" mentality, they will continue to struggle to crack this ever growing (and very lucrative) market. For example, if the company is in the business of creating accounting software for larger businesses and giant corporations, it must come up with a completely different marketing strategy in order to sell that same software to small business leaders.

Remember, they believe they are special; they are "different," but in a good way… simply because they are a small business leader. They are proud of who they are, the business they run, and the profits they make each month.

So, stop treating them like another corporate customer, and the company will have a chance at bringing them on board.

**Not identifying the target audience: small businesses fall into various categories: 1-10 employees, 11-25 employees, 26-50 employees, etc.** How does the company's marketing department team go about identifying their small business prospects? Do they put them all together in one category, and hope for the best? If they do, failure is bound to result, and you may have experienced that scenario already. But don't fear; there is a cure! And it all begins with very careful planning.

Believe it or not, small business owners think both the same, and differently, depending upon the size of their company. In other words, a small business owner who only has five employees will think twice, if not three times, before deciding to purchase a product or service. But compare that to a small business owner who has 30 to 35 or more employees; they have already experienced growth, and even though they will still be "very careful" with their spending habits, they are more likely to say "yes" than the small business owner who has five or fewer employees. Do the math; it does make sense… and then create a marketing campaign designed to meet the small business owner where they are.

**The product is too complicated to be installed or used by a small business owner.** Want to know the secret to "repeat sales" when it comes to the small business sector? Keep everything simple; keep instructions as "easy as possible" to read and understand. Small business owners are very busy people; they do not have time to waste, nor do they want their employees to waste time trying to learn how to operate a complicated product or service. When corporate marketing experts learn what small business owners are looking for, especially when it comes to "instructions and information," they will reap the benefits of their efforts.

**Buying the product requires the small business owner and their employees to spend too much time on your product or service.** Again, we cannot emphasize this point enough: to a small business owner, "time is money." So if the product or service requires the small business owner or their key employees to spend too much of their time to meet the demands of your marketing pitch, you have lost the sale. Keep it simple!

**The product or service demands the small business owner to "change."** If there is any group of people on the planet that resist the word "change," it is the small business sector. For various reasons, change is a word they do not want to hear about. To them, change means "problems will result," and no small business owner wants to bring in new problems that will affect their bottom line. How can you get around this obstacle? Simple: when putting together your promotion and marketing campaign, stress the "positive benefits" they will experience by coming on board as a customer. Minimize any reference to the word change and make it easy for them.

**The price benefit model does not work well for a small business audience.** Small business owners and executives do not work well with a standard "corporate" model of how they will benefit from using your product or service. In other words, you must convince them that by coming on board as a customer with your corporation they will save money, reduce expenses, and increase their bottom line. While those might seem like impossible tasks to put together, a savvy marketing expert who knows the small business sector better than anyone else can accomplish those goals.

**The product or service is not easily understood.** One of the biggest obstacles to face as a "marketing expert" is creating a campaign and information about the product or service that is "easy as 1-2-3." Most corporate marketing campaigns targeted to the small business sector fail miserably because their information, advertisements and promotional materials are written in what seems like "a foreign language." So, how do your company's marketing materials and campaigns measure up? Is the information easy to read and understand? Or, does it raise more questions than answers?

**The product or service requires too long of a time period before they see a return on their investment.** Small business owners and leaders need to see an "immediate" return on their investment. And that is probably an unusual way of thinking to most corporate marketing "experts." For example, a corporate sales person can convince another corporate customer that they will see a "return on their investment in 18 months to two years." And those corporate customers will usually nod and say, "Okay, you made the sale."

But, if you try to explain to a small business owner they need to wait for that long of a time frame, they will not hesitate to show the salesperson the door. So, adjust the corporate way of thinking, and come up with a campaign that will convince the small business owner that they will indeed "reap the return on their investment" in a very short period of time. Weeks, not months, works best for selling to the small business sector.

**The product or service is simply a "substitute" for an existing one, and not really perceived as being necessary.** What exactly is it you are trying to sell to the small business sector? Is it something new? Is it something they will really believe they "cannot live without?" Or, is your product or service just a rehash of something that is already on the market? The small business owner has one simple philosophy: "if it ain't broke, don't fix it." In other words, if the product or service they are currently using is working out for them, they will see no logical need to try something new…. unless he or she can be convinced otherwise.

**The product or service is "too early in the change process."** We already addressed the issue of how small business owners do not like change. And when it comes to trying something "new," they do not really want to be "first." They would prefer that other small businesses try a new product or service, and see how it worked for them. One surefire way to get new small business clients on board is by having the company's product or service tested by other small business owners. Even if it means giving away products or services, in the end the positive "word of mouth" experience will work wonders for your campaign.

What is true is that small business leaders need to feel that the product or service offering is designed with their operations in mind from the ground up. It is not enough to tell a business leader that the product worked well for a Fortune 1000 corporation. They want to make doubly sure it will work for their enterprise – whether it is five employees or 55 staff members.

## Success Factors

Four major reasons offerings are not small market successes include:

➜ The installation time, materials and costs are too much for smaller enterprises.
➜ Oftentimes, other parts of the company need to be changed to

accommodate the new product or service.

➤ Employees feel antagonistic to new ideas, even if it will make their jobs easier, and the training is arduous.

➤ The cost of the new product or service outweighs the benefits or Return On Investment (ROI).

The first Internet bubble showed all of these negatives in stark detail. Small businesses could not participate because the technology did not exist for them to easily install or operate systems or products.

As we mentioned earlier, the second wave, called 2.0, is considered a difficult transition for many small businesses. But it is marked by much easier to use and implement products that often run on the Internet instead of on the firm's hardware.

Having given all these negatives, let's talk about ways to succeed because this book is about success – the company's.

Small business owners are slow adapters but once the value proposition is proven, they are willing to make the commitment.

A good example of this trend and how it is impacting smaller companies is eCommerce. Put simply, eCommerce represents the logical migration to the Internet of catalogs and buying portals. At the turn of the century, eCommerce applications were cumbersome, needed heavy customization and significant support. One such application was the shopping cart that enables visitors to browse and buy in an electronic storefront.

Today, while it is relatively easy to install a "shopping cart" application to allow a small-size enterprise to accept payment on the web, it does require significant commitment of resources by small businesses. However, as the selling landscape has changed and Internet-based sales are growing in importance, small business leaders recognize that they must adapt or suffer lower sales volumes.

In 2008, one out of six respondents to ISI's surveys said they were considering or had installed a web-based 2.0 equivalent application. In 2009, the number doubled, and it is expected to continue exponentially.

Marketers should study this example as a reference point. The reason 2.0 applications are catching on? They are:

→ Easier to install, learn and apply than previous offerings.
→ Less costly.
→ Tested by other small firms and recommended.
→ Simplified applications, better support and better marketing efforts on the part of providers.

Shopping carts demonstrate the pluses and minuses of small business marketing. If a product can help them grow and does not change the way they do business, small business leaders will adapt. The key is demonstrating this proposition and showing that others are doing it successfully.

Let's talk about these key product characteristics in turn.

Products and services succeed in the small business space because they mimic current usage and practices. There is little time lost by company staff learning how to use these tools: electronic, print, physical or financial. The reason Intuit's products are so readily accepted is that they mimic what individuals and companies are doing, only more efficiently.

There must be an obvious cost savings in time *and* money to make them popular with small business leaders. It is not enough that products saves time, they also must be less costly than the product or service they replace. *ADP* succeeds in payroll accounting because the money and time saved far outweighs the initial costs of switching over.

Testing products and services before they reach market is a key component of any product development cycle. Moreover, the testers must also be willing to recommend the products or services. One new 2.0 product we worked with failed because it was rushed to market without testing. Only when it was installed in several client operations did the developers learn that it gobbled up too much computer resources or RAM, forcing users to purchase additional computing capacity. This problem would have surfaced, had they tested. Also, initial users were not happy and they were vocal in their criticism.

Another key component of good product development is following that old rule: KISS – Keep It Simple, Stupid.

Venture capitalists put a premium on the "elevator pitch." Essentially, can the product/service be described in 25 words or less and is it instantly understandable? More importantly, does the product/service apply to the small business leader's enterprise?

For companies looking to generate new sales Victor Cheng has an interesting, effective approach – books. More specifically, he helps a company to produce a book written by a senior manager, usually President or CEO, that is designed to display the firm's abilities in the target sector.

Cheng's pitch is simple – "my company will help your company grow using your own expertise to generate sales." His company has criteria that staffers use to judge if a company is in the so-called "sweet spot" for a Bookmercial, which just happens to be the name of his firm. He argues that such an approach can be a powerful credibility building and revenue-generating marketing tool.

Support is another key component of any product/service offering. Vonage failed to exploit its initial success as a VoIP (Voice over Internet Protocol) because its support was poor and angered many subscribers. On the other hand, American Express does a remarkable job of supporting its premium level cards such as the Platinum and Black. Support needs to be a short telephone call away and service with a smile a watchword.

This brings us to a pet peeve of many small business owners – having support come from India, China or the Philippines. Selling to an audience that for the most part makes its living on American commerce requires a feeling that the seller is also focusing on US efforts. Having call centers in foreign locales may be cost effective but it is not sales-effective.

Winston Churchill said "America and Britain are separated by a common language." Indians do not speak American English and they, and other nationals, follow a proscribed procedure, often to the dismay of the client.

Small business leaders do not waste time and when they need to repeat name, customer number and other details several times, it becomes frustrating. Particularly if they are forced to repeat procedures already tried before calling customer support.

The final leg of product development is the marketing of the product/service itself. This is detailed in later chapters but one overriding mantra must be observed – develop a product for the small business sector and don't downsize a big corporation offering.

One key characteristic that makes for success is to insure that the product/service replaces an existing activity with little money and less hassle.

A marketer using the *Janus Principle* approach will appreciate all of these factors in creating a product or service for the small business marketplace. At the same time, he or she will need to contend with a lot of internal factors in bringing a product or service to the small business marketplace, not the least of which will be the pricing for such offerings. This brings us to the other part of product development – pricing.

## Pricing the Product to the Audience

Pricing a product or service is always a tricky endeavor. On one side, the temptation is to keep the price as high as possible in order to enjoy the best profits possible. However, the small business sector is different from the usual corporate clients. Whereas the large company is used to dealing with bigger corporate clients, the small business customer is different. It needs creative pricing strategies that make the product/service affordable for them to buy.

Pricing is where the *Janus Principle* is often most important.

Many companies decide to go ahead with a product/service based on an ROI (Return on Investment) that is amortized quickly, or worse they need to double their return. This tendency is not limited to large corporations.

One smaller IT supplier created a web portal for a large client, then turned around and tried to create a small business product in which it factored in the original development costs into its pricing model. In short, they were trying to get back the development costs twice. As a result, their pricing for the small business market was almost the same as if they were selling to a single large corporate client.

Pricing strategies need to reflect an understanding that small business leaders like to (and must) conserve cash. So, the more "creative and out of the box" style pricing options offered to them, the better the outcome for everyone involved.

## The Payback Model

Many large companies look at small businesses as the "low hanging fruit," and oftentimes mistakenly believe that the traditional model in which a corporate client doesn't mind waiting two years or longer to recoup their investment is the right one. However, as we have mentioned numerous times, *the small business sector does not operate like the usual corporate client!*

A small business leader who needs to purchase products or services will look at affordability, creative financing options, and a return on their investment in twelve months or less. When you consider creating a pricing model that gives the small business sector what they are really looking for, you, the marketer will succeed.

Think of it in terms of "relationship building." In other words, if you become someone the small business leader or executive can trust, you will win them over as a new customer. Build a working relationship that makes it a "win-win" situation for both parties, and you will have a new customer for life, versus a large corporate customer whose employees have 2-3 year tenure. It may sound like it is too good to be true, but there are countless success stories of corporations who took time to establish relationships and built trust with small business clients.

At the same time, however, there are also countless stories of failure, from major corporations who just didn't "get it." They weren't able to understand how the small business leader could serve as a partner in their endeavors, and therefore a key factor to their success was missed.

The company's pricing strategy must include value pricing which appeals to the basic need of a small business leader: "to conserve cash." Make that happen, and the sale is made; it is simple as that. The pricing strategy must also allow the small business leader to invest as minimally as possible in the beginning. When that happens, it creates a "bond" between the buyer and the seller. For example, some companies will offer "bargain basement" opportunities: a direct mail company may offer up to 500 names and addresses for a mere twenty-five dollars. If the small business leader has a good experience with that initial offering, they will explore other offers from that same company in the near future.

The company must do everything in its power to win over the small business sector. Work *with* them, and not *against* them, and garner the sale.

## Payment Options

**Offer Leasing and Payment Arrangements That Stretch Out Financing.** *Dell Inc.* is the perfect example of how a major corporation has "cracked the code" and learned how to sell computer systems and services to the small business sector. The *Dell* computer ads are virtually everywhere. And those ads offer plenty of leasing options for the consumer and the small business sector as well.

When the company offers leasing opportunities and creative payment options to a small business leader, he or she will view it as an opportunity to conserve their cash. And if the company's reputation in the marketplace is a sound one, they will be tempted to give the product or service a try thereby creating a positive working relationship.

**Accept Credit Cards.** Many small businesses use credit cards to take advantage of frequent flier miles, free gifts and other rewards. And while they do have a preference for buying products and services with a credit card, most will pay off the balance within thirty to sixty days.

Most small business leaders and executives view credit cards as the "trusted plastic" method. While many will not use this option for major purchases, it is another checkpoint in their discovery process. Credit cards act as cash reserves for many small business leaders.

**Calculate Pricing in a Way That Ensures Maximum Support.** Many corporate marketing experts fail to recognize how important "service and support" really is to the small business sector. If the company adds a "free" component that covers support and service, and truly means it (without any hidden costs or fees), then word will quickly spread throughout the small business community, and it will become a name trusted in their world.

Do not make the mistake of thinking service and support is just sending a small business leader to a website for information, especially in those annoying "frequently asked questions" format. And do not make the mistake of outsourcing the service to a company that operates outside of the United States. As we said earlier, small business leaders are a loyal group and they think locally and talk with someone who speaks their language – American English.

There are two interesting trends we have noted. One is that many companies are offering a Spanish alternative to callers.

The second is the tier phone service approach. *American Express* makes sure its Platinum and Black members talk with someone in the U.S. That is not necessarily the case for its Gold and Green credit cards. Interestingly, its small business cards are serviced from overseas, a mistake we think and small business leaders have also told us so.

## Create Pricing That Permits Substitution

By creating pricing options that allow a small business client to make substitutions as they see fit, the company is increasing the chances of making a sale. In other words, will the small business leader truly believe they will make or save any money by using the products or services? Or will they believe it will cost them, not only in terms of putting cash up front, but also in terms of time, frustration and headaches?

The small business leader or executive must be convinced that whatever is being offered to them will "change their world" for the better, and ultimately, increase their bottom line (in the shortest time possible).

## Keep Initial Pricing Affordable

Another strategy we cannot stress enough is this: small business leaders are not pioneers! When it comes to parting with their hard earned cash, they will hang on to it as long as possible.

One key to pricing is to demonstrate clearly what the total cost for the product or service will be. Small business leaders do not like surprises. They certainly do not want open-ended charges that do not have a cap.

These leaders also want finite contracts with the ability to opt-out at given points with total obligations clearly spelled out.

In surveys and working with marketers, *ISI* thinks the threshold for most companies is $400 a month for any goods or services with little or no up-front installation fees. Barring that, they prefer a full-package price that gives leadership. The threshold here is $4,000.

Price your products or services so that initial sales will convince your target audience that yours is the one they should try. Don't price yourself too high, but instead, price it low enough to make it enticing to them. Keep it simple, build trust, and over the long haul, you can add more products and services and make your marketing efforts pay off.

Every product and every service has the potential to appeal to a wide audience. But the company's task is to learn as much as possible about the small business sector *before* creating a campaign that will succeed.

The amount of time spent on market research, getting to know and understand the small business world, especially how they operate on shoestring budgets and creative pricing options, will be worth it in the long term.

## Experiment with Short Paid Programs

Short paid programs and/or free trials, under the proper conditions, are an effective marketing tool. After first identifying marketing segments for which the short paid offering is an effective sales pitch, make it so attractive that they cannot say "no." If the product or service really is that good, and the price is just right, they will have a hard time turning it down. For examples, be sure to visit the websites of *Intuit, Lowe's, Staples, Pitney Bowes* and other major retailers where small business leaders and managers are customers.

However a pricing decision is made, think of the marketplace mores first and not the corporate pricing patterns in order to be successful. Equally as important, prepare the company to absorb, promote and support the pricing algorithms. This is putting the *Janus Principle* to work in a key area.

## The Pricing Game

"Pricing is a game" a marketing executive told us. In fact, he explained the pricing game so well, we quote him below.

"Like the Janus concept it involves two groups, the company and the clients," he said. "Before I even think about what the selling price is, I need to worry about the internal bean counters. They set up ROI goals, spending limits and a host of other factors that make the price seem a matter of picking up a formula.

"Then there are the outside forces: my competitors and my clients. Before I can look at what my customers will pay, I need to see what my competitors are charging.

"Once I see their prices, I can see what the customer will pay.

"After all is said and done, pricing is as much a science as an art and my audiences are both inside and outside the company."

While pricing is important to a small business buyer, it is not the only variable.

# THE WHERE

In talking with the Senior Vice President of a nationally known brand in the office products space, he told us that reaching small business leaders was his toughest challenge.

"If I could only get them to listen to my story, they would buy my product," he lamented.

As we probed deeper, we discovered that:

→ His advertising and promotion budget to generate leads was divided roughly into 60% national, 35% regional and 5% local media venues.

→ His main personal contact points were national chains such as Staples, Office Depot and Office Max.

→ This executive's brand competed on price and productivity enhancement while providing effective merchandising tools to his retailers.

→ Within his competitive space, there was no clear brand leader and little word-of-mouth "buzz."

→ Our research showed, however, that his century old brand was known to 70% of small business leaders surveyed.

In recommending a marketing solution, we took a page from former House Speaker John W. McCormack. A product of Massachusetts ward politics, that crusty politician emphasized that "all politics are local." And that's what we told this manager to do. Start at the local level.

For him and many other companies, a national brand needs a national media outlet. Small business leaders think locally when it comes to purchasing decisions. This dichotomy is another example of the need for a *Janus Principle* approach.

Happily for this client's company, he looked at both sides of the equation and asked us: "How do I do it?" While not simple, it can be done. We will explain a little bit later. Before we do, however, let's look at the "Where" in more detail and in terms of the *Janus Principle*.

## Finding The Right Channels

Because the small business sector is so huge and so diverse, it is often difficult to find the right channels to reach its leaders. Ironically, we touch those channels everyday but don't see them for what they are – effective communication and sales nodes. Seeing and using these channels is often key to adding customers and opening new markets.

The best form of communications is the in-person touch. Unfortunately, personal contact is waning in this age of Internet, telephone and direct mail *vis-à-vis* the small business leader. And that is unfortunate because it is still the best form of communication. As one expert said, communications is 55% body language; 38% voice tone and 7% words. An in-person encounter encompasses all three elements.

The demise of the local distributor and salesperson on a route is to be lamented. This individual played an important role in maintaining a close personal relationship between client and supplier. Today, phone centers, many of them placed overseas, are used as substitutes for personal contact and sales. Together with the Internet and direct mail, they represent the bulk of a company's contact with small business leaders.

A lot of big corporations complain, "I can't afford to sell to small businesses." But they have it totally backwards. They should understand that they "cannot afford *not* to sell to small businesses," which make up a very large portion of the economic picture in the United States and their company's potential customer base.

# The Personal Approach

In order to successfully crack the small business marketplace, the company must position itself to make an effective first approach, one that includes some sort of "personal approach." The Internet and phone calling are starting points but a small business leader needs to be stroked, courted, wined and dined. And they must feel that they are getting "special service" before they will consider making a purchase. Many corporations feel that the cost of sales to do this is prohibitive. We argue that the cost of failure is too great not to do this.

Just recently we were working with a New Orleans promotion company run by two of the smartest women we know. One of the questions they asked us was "Do I need to email or write immediately after returning to the office after a sales call?" After a moment of stunned silence, an *ISI* staffer replied – "If you want the sale you will need to."

Small business leaders are "very careful" about gathering relevant data, information and facts before making any decision regarding the purchasing of products or services. Remember, to a small business leader, "time is money," so while major corporations won't hesitate to shell out thousands of dollars on a new purchase after only a few minutes of learning about the product or service, the same does not hold true for the small business market.

*ISI* has found that the local independent drug store is now one of the last bastions of individual leadership with perceived wisdom. These locations are filling the role of the local hardware, stationary, grocery and barbershop in dispensing purchasing advice.

A small consulting firm with its own building in Cliffside Park, New Jersey suffered catastrophic flooding, which forced them to look for a plumber. Given the poor reputation of many plumbers in their locale, they sought advice. The best suggestion and ultimate choice came from their local druggist.

That druggist in turn spent two years installing a prescription management system, which caused significant heartache. As the druggist told the authors, "I didn't listen to others in the area but went with a system that was touted by a supplier. It cost me thousands before they got it right."

For information gathering, local organizations are also very important to a small business leader. Whether it's the local Kiwanis, Rotary or Chamber of Commerce, small business leaders, who see themselves as the "business leaders" feel a real connection at those meetings and events.

Keep in mind, people will ask their friends for recommendations when they need a plumber, roofer, mechanic or other service repair person. And they take those recommendations very seriously. Small business leaders are no different, and they will not hesitate to ask their friends and business associates for referrals, information and data that will fill their needs and wants. *And many of those referrals are found at local gatherings!*

In Connecticut, the state's largest insurance company was an early proponent of health savings accounts (a consumer-directed healthcare option) and utilized the state Chamber of Commerce to inform, communicate and ultimately sell these policies.

So where are the best places to sell small business leaders? The very best place is at his or her place of business.

The personal visit is the best venue for the company's sales pitch, provided the salesperson has done his or her homework. Unfortunately, many companies believe that the phone and Internet are sufficient in this process. The drill today is to call and have the target audience go online so that they can watch a demonstration or program while the individual talks. Cost efficient? Yes! Most effective? No!

For that office supply executive. Our solution fas the following:

- **From his sales records we asked him to pick a neighborhood of office complexes in New Jersey and Pennsylvania.**
- **We then redirected his telephone team to setting up appointments for his regional manager and one sales person to set up 15-minute appointments with business leaders for a three-day period.**
- **At the same time, his communications group called the local Chamber of Commerce, Rotary, Kiwanis and other business groups offering to provide a speaker for an event around the same time.**
- **Concurrently, the local Staples, Office Max and Office Depot stores were offered a special merchandising promotion to run two weeks before and two weeks after the visits.**

As a result of these efforts, the company had 21 appointments, two speaking engagements and a special promotion in Office Max in Pennsylvania and about the same in southern New Jersey. When all of this was completed, the sales of its products were monitored for two months prior and three months subsequent to the effort.

The result? 19% gain in product sales for the two months following the event. More importantly, sales remained high throughout the remainder of the year in the Pennsylvania area at the Staples store and rose at the other locations as well.

This effort succeeded because the combination of personal visits, public speaking and promotion worked. Each reinforced the message and brought it down to the local level.

Not every company can do something like this but the lessons it implies can be applied elsewhere.

One other thing we learned from this experience and others is that what is said and done in the personal interaction between marketer and buyer is more important than one might think.

## Keys To Success

A successful marketer once gave us the keys to success. When talking to small business leaders he always:

→ Talked in their language or "tribal words."
→ Sought their input first, and never talked about his product until they asked.
→ Looked to solve their problems, needs.
→ Always used a local reference in talking about his product.
→ Followed up; followed up; followed up.
→ Made customer service a priority.

In this chapter, we have recommended significant changes in the way a company looks at the small business marketplace. It is one of the lessons we learned on the way to postulating the *Janus Principle*.

In fact, it was only when we turned our company upside down

and looked inward at what we did that we were able to become a leading information source to small business leaders. Our company now talks to hundreds of small business leaders every month, solicits their thoughts, asks for referrals, and does many of the things we are recommending herein. As a result, we have become successful in this sector.

Our next chapter talks about the communication between seller and buyer but keep these thoughts in mind. They include:

→ The personal touch is important.
→ Learn about the company first.
→ Identify the influencers.
→ Talk in the tribal words of the audience.
→ Understand their needs and address them.

# THE WHEN

As the Bible says: There is a season. A time to be born. A time to die. A time to plant. A time to reap.

For large corporations, the year is divided into starting new projects in the first quarter. The second and third quarters are devoted to selling and producing. In the last quarter, the emphasis is on "making the numbers" and cleaning up projects.

To most small business leaders, there are no seasons, just the daily grind of getting out the product or service, collecting the monies owed and insuring that the business can continue.

For the small business leader, his or her business day is focused on getting the product or service out the door. They spend most of their time supervising or monitoring the "day to day" operations of their business. Often times they are "putting out fires," and solving problem after problem.

## The "After Hour" Sale

In *ISI*'s surveys over the years, point to a conclusion that the buy decision for products or services is often made after hours by small business leaders. One *Staples* store manager in the Midwest noted that he saw small business employees in his store during the day but business leaders after 8 pm.

A small business leader is too busy during the day to make important decisions regarding purchasing any new products or services. All of his or her time and attention is devoted to making sure the business runs smoothly. No matter how many people they have working for them, they still understand that "the buck starts and stops" at their desk. They feel responsible for the health and heartbeat of their organization, and will not often be bothered listening to sales people who try to pitch their products or services to them during normal business hours.

In the evenings, when things finally settle down, small business leaders will then consider reading sales materials, brochures, e-mails, and other promotional items. They perceive this time of the night to be "just right" for those types of decisions that have to be made.

Weekends and holiday are also extensions of the work week for most small business leaders. When the telephones aren't ringing and there are no fires to put out, they take the time to gather and review information, and then make their buy decisions. Smart marketers make it easier for the small business leader to access, absorb, and query your offering. That is why it is important to have the information on the website and your home or cellular number on your business card.

## Contrasts In Decision Making

Before we go further, let's contrast this with when and where a large organization makes decisions.

As we said earlier, a large organization manager spends a great deal of time building consensus. These activities occur during the day, in the office, on the smoking dock and in the lunchroom. He or she devotes efforts to communicating with others within the organization. A small business leader spends time talking with peers and others outside the organization, after hours or at meetings about a purchasing decision. He or she also spends time on weekends and holidays working at his or her business.

In our surveys, employees of larger corporations spend a significant time dealing with internal issues. By contrast, small business leaders focus on the operations and growth of their enterprises.

These types of contrasts drove us to identify the need for and develop the basics of the *Janus Principle*. This dichotomy is one reason we focus on the when and where marketers should deliver their message to small business leaders.

Now let's move on further and look at the way small business leaders go about the buy decision.

## The Buy Decision

Small business leaders, our surveys show, do not initiate 80% of their purchasing efforts. Rather these efforts are triggered by a negative outcome either in terms of sales or in operations. When an event occurs, the small business leader begins to seek alternatives.

A common scenario is when a system failure loses valuable data and there is no back-up. There is the old adage about getting fire extinguishers after the barn has burned down and the horse has escaped. Many firms purchase back-up systems only after they have suffered a significant data loss.

During this phase the small business leader may use generic search terms related to the product or services sought in order to form a short list of potential providers.

Later, in the evaluation stage of the buying cycle, the purchaser's focus turns from researching potential suppliers to researching specific issues related to the product or service, such as performance, efficiency, maintenance, ergonomics and White Papers.

Usually, the next step is to ask peers or other business managers for advice.

These two activities represent 90% of the effort to identify specific resources to solve this particular problem. Finding suppliers reverses the process with personal recommendations taking the most prominent role. In both cases, these activities take place either during break times (lunch) or after work.

Our studies have shown that whereas corporate managers spend

30-40% of their day identifying and sourcing, small business leaders spend less than 10%. Only after the small business leader has a thorough understanding of specific needs, wants, and issues affecting the purchase decision, does he or she devote their valuable business hours to the process.

In this scenario, the role of the company's off-line and on-line efforts become critical to insuring that it will be in the final stages (the purchasing step) of this process.

In the "How" section of this book, we go into great detail about what the company needs to do: seven touches.

For now it is important to remember that, in general, there needs to be at least seven touches in order to motivate a small business leader to buy. By touches, we mean putting the company's name and product/service in front of potential buyers. These touches can comprise any combination of print, broadcast, out-of-office, Internet and personal contact. Based on our experience, the more personal and directed these touches tend to be, the better. How personal can one get in the sales process?

In the New York City area, we know of a salesperson who calls up potential clients and says: "Let me bring you a corned beef sandwich from *Katz's Delicatessen* and talk about your company and its needs." He claims a hit ratio of about 25% using this approach, particularly among Jewish clients who know about *Katz's*.

Why is this approach successful? As he says, "Everybody's got to eat. Most of my clients eat in every day and I bring them something different. For 15 bucks I am in the door."

We talk much about the Rotary and Kiwanis and other service clubs because they are an excellent venue for meeting potential clients. But even here, the emphasis must be on education and not sales. Lawyers, accountants and financial advisors have long used these venues to find clients. They are equally fertile for office supplies, insurance, cartage, equipment rental, IT support, telephone sales and a host of other products/services.

The best way to use these venues is as speakers. Bringing in a regional executive to talk about the state of the telephone industry and offering a free month's trial to the audience is an example of how one new communications firm debuted in several Pennsylvania counties.

# Direct Mail Still Works

While direct mail is losing favor among small business marketers as they switch to email marketing, there is still a strong role in the process for it. Small business leaders read direct mail, if however briefly, in their location during the day and review those that are put aside at night. Equally as important, direct mail is printed material that is often brought out days, weeks and even months later.

We discuss how to plan, create and distribute direct mail in later sections. Suffice it to say that direct mail is a very effective tool in small business marketing. The proof of the pudding is that many major marketers still use this media heavily.

From the distribution of our newsletters, we have noticed a trend over the years and reflected in five million mailings a month. Small business leaders open their mail primarily in the morning before 8:30 am and after 6 pm in the evening. This pattern holds true as we move across the country's time zones. In the western states the early hours may reflect the work habits, which start at 8 am in most of these locales and end at 5 pm. Nonetheless, the pattern holds true.

In contrast, managers who are in bigger corporations open their mail at all hours with the heaviest concentration at the 8-9 am time frame. In comparison to small business leaders, few open emails at night.

Small business leaders know when their busy times are during the year. Many will tell a salesperson that he or she is always busy. There is some validity in that because they tend to take fewer, more concentrated vacations. (By the way, they tend to spend more than their counterparts in large corporations.)

Companies tend to launch products around industry shows or in the beginning of the year. Small business leaders shop year-round, hindered only by their high stress times. If there is seasonality, it is November and December, when small business leaders determine their cash flow for the year and if it is prudent, from a tax point-of-view, invest in equipment or other necessities. Like white sales (for linens and sheets) in January for consumers, small business leaders tell us that they often get better deals from suppliers trying to make end-of-year quotas.

For some, this is also a time of frustration when they want to do a deal and the sellers are preoccupied with year-end closings and parties.

This brings us to another "when." Year-end holidays.

Small business owners appreciate the holiday greetings, calendars and other traditional communications that accompany year-end happenings. In fact, our studies show, they are more likely to remember these contacts in the New Year.

Calendar makers tell us that volume has decreased over the years as costs to purchase and send these traditional handouts have risen significantly. But think of the benefit, a company's name, logo on the wall and seen 300+ days a year. It is interesting that if one visits a small business there will always be a calendar from a supplier on the wall. In a large corporation, one hardly sees such reminders.

We have now gone through the Why, Who, What, Where and When of marketing to small business leaders. Since execution is the key to any successful venture, we will devote the rest of this book to the "How" of small business marketing.

# THE HOW

At Harvard Business School, they teach students that execution is the key to success. Venture capitalists consider the management team the key ingredient in deciding whether they will invest in an enterprise. We devote a large section of this book to the "How" of small business marketing because it is in the execution that small business marketers need to excel.

Successful marketing companies try to understand what their customers need, figure out better ways to build a promise that meets that need, and fulfill it. These are some marketing questions we ask our clients and ourselves:

- ➜ Who are our ideal small business customers?
- ➜ How much revenue do these small business customers bring us over time?
- ➜ How much of those dollars is available to invest in winning more small business customers like this?
- ➜ Where are all of the rest of the small business people like this who are not buying from us?
- ➜ How can we invest in programs that will begin a relationship with these small business people in a way that will measurably activate our sales process?
- ➜ How will we measure and report impact of marketing programs'

dollars on inquiry, lead, appointment, presentation, proposal and sale levels?

→ What is the average time it takes to move a relationship from inquiry to sale?

→ How far do we need to take it?

If you can answer these questions, you are well on your way to making much better marketing investments that will bring you a measurable ROI.

For some companies, there is an arrogance bred of success. This arrogance spills over into their marketing efforts and can be both a virtue and a curse.

We identified the *Janus Principle* as an outgrowth of our work with many corporate clients. Some have come to us after being humbled by the small business marketplace. Others continue to make the same mistakes over and over again.

The "How" of small business marketing requires many of us to suspend our own prejudices and arrogance, and look at this audience in different ways. Much of the "How" is Basic Marketing 101. But it is surprising how many of us neglect the lessons learned in basic courses in the marketing effort.

Perhaps the most important lesson to learn about small business marketing is to eliminate the word "I" from our vocabulary and substitute the word "You."

## The "I" Of Selling Should Be Replaced By The "You" Of Success

In a study for one large corporate client of 24 small business websites, 250 direct mail pieces and listening to hundreds of sales presentations, our staffers found that a majority of marketers talk about themselves first, the product second and the benefits to the listener a distant third.

While it certainly reflects the "me-first" generation, it doesn't make for good small business marketing. The "I" in small business marketing should be replaced by the "you" of smart selling.

Eleanor Roosevelt had an interesting way of judging people. She simply waited for how long it took her conversation companion to say the word "I." The longer it took, the better she liked the person.

Small business leaders most often judge the sales call on how well the salesperson knows their company and their needs. Unfortunately, many marketers and sales people don't bother to find out what are the key elements of their target audiences. Big companies and start-up entrepreneurs all make the same mistake. They concentrate on establishing themselves and their product before determining what the client needs.

Having established the climate in which small business leaders view purchasing products and services, let us now discuss ways of getting a small business leader to buy your product or service.

## Are You Selling What Your Potential Client is Buying?

One of the most common faults that we at *ISI* find with marketing and sales campaigns is that there seems to be a lack of understanding of what the marketing and sales people should be trying to accomplish.

When we talk to marketing and sales people about what they are trying to accomplish we have found that their whole strategy of reaching the small business customer is not very defined. "I have a small business offering for you" will not do it. This approach is too vague and is not at all confidence-inspiring for the target client. There has to be focus in your marketing and sales campaigns as well as in all the tools that you are employing. To be successful in your campaigns you have to understand the basic fundamentals of the sale.

There are several key elements to every successful sales presentation. Eliminating or neglecting these elements almost assures that your presentation will not end with your objective.

Two of the essential elements are: *Establishing Need* and *Creating Value*. Leave out either of these steps and you make closing the sale extremely difficult.

## Establishing Need

First, it may seem obvious, but establishing need is a key ingredient. Obtaining a sale is not about trying to sell your potential customer what you think they need. What you should be doing is discovering what their needs are. You should not be telling your prospective customer what his or her needs should be. People do not buy for your reasons; they buy for their own reasons.

The key to establishing need is determining what's important to your prospective customer. This must be your aim and you must use your entire presentation to meet that objective. *Webster's Dictionary* defines "aim" as moving toward a specified goal or objective. It is imperative that you move toward discovering what your client perceives the problem to be; then explain how you can meet that need. Don't waste time telling prospective customers what you think they want to hear. Find out what your target wants and deliver it to them. It is much easier to sell what small business leaders are buying.

Establishing need requires you to be observant, you must *learn* from your prospective customer. Listen to what the prospective customer tells you. To successfully uncover need you must listen and listen carefully. Listen through the ears of the potential client. Hear what he or she is telling you.

Erase any preconceived notions about why you think your prospective customer will buy and concentrate on what he or she is telling you they will buy.

Ask questions which open up discussions about the prospective customer's needs and what he or she is expecting to accomplish.
Repeat your prospective customer's needs often to ensure you are hearing what (s)he is saying and to help you stay focused and on track.

Never take a prospective customer's need lightly. If it is important to them then it better be important to you. The prospective customer's needs are the reason he or she will buy.

## Creating Value

Creating value is showing how you can meet the prospective

customer's needs, desires and expectations. As your prospective customer shares what they are hoping the offering will do for them, you should be making mental notes of how your offering can fulfill those needs. Make sure the prospective customers understand exactly how they will benefit personally. Value is only created when the prospective customer sees how he or she, and ultimately their company, is going to personally benefit from purchasing the offering. Value is not created in a generic sense, but in a very real, personal sense.

Need and value are inseparably linked; you cannot establish one without the other.

Many marketers think the value comes from the product/service and that new is better, more profitable for the purchaser. Substitution is often the mantra of the marketer rather than profit improvement. In our surveys of small business leaders we have found that small business owners have just the opposite feeling. They go more by the adage of "if it ain't broke, don't fix it."

The experience of *Microsoft's* Vista operating system is a good example of this. While the company won't release figures, industry experts believe that adoption by small business leaders, a prime market, is well below the company's expectations. Our own surveys show that just one in ten business leaders said they had bought or were considering adopting this new operating system. Put another way, more than 45% of all small business leaders responding said they were still operating with Windows 98 (brought out in the 1990s). One in three said they were still using PCs bought before the turn of the century.

*Microsoft's* answer to this reluctance to change was to announce that it would stop supporting Windows 98. This approach is one reason why the company is consistently rated poorly in *ISI's* surveys of suppliers.

On the other hand, *FedExKinko's* is viewed as the most popular supplier precisely because its employees speak to small business leaders every day. This popularity continues despite the fact that the cost of using their services has gone up an average 14% since 2004.

When asked why they had not upgraded their systems, more than 70% said that they saw no need, as current resources were "good enough."

The nation's press is bombarding small business leaders with the advantages of 2.0 and other new innovations. Yet, small business leaders stubbornly stick to older technology because basically it works and they are concentrating on other parts of their business like selling and delivering their goods and services.

Remember, they were bitten badly by the advent of broadband and many small business leaders are loath to make another technology mistake.

We highlighted this earlier that the 2.0 application of the shopping cart was being adopted because of pressure from buyers who are using the Internet more for purchasing. This example clearly documents the fact that small business leaders are conservative when it comes to purchases. Therefore, marketers must find effective ways of reaching and selling them. Whether you are a big company or a new entrepreneur, just because they are innovators doesn't mean small business leaders accept the innovations of others.

## Critical Sell Points

There are three things that our surveys find critical to selling into this marketplace:

*Very important:* You need to have a "third party" endorsement from another satisfied small business leader as one of your primary marketing efforts. In other words, find a small business leader who has used your product or service and has been "extremely pleased," and use their comments and testimonials. A word or two from another small business user will influence many other small business leaders to come on board.

*Another important point:* You must remember to sell the "benefit, benefit and benefit" of the product, and NOT the product itself.

*And finally:* Do not expect to influence small business leaders with big names like Warren Buffet or Donald Trump; you'll get more of a response by using a small business user to say, "I used it, and I highly recommend it." It is a myth that the bigger the endorser, the more potent the message.

For many marketers, all of the above is difficult to assimilate but is important to winning the small business leader's attention and closing the sale. And the buyer's attention window is getting smaller. We have become a "15-minute world" according to experts, and marketers must adjust to that dynamic. This means the seller needs to get to the heart of the sale quicker, proffer the benefits and stop dwelling on themselves. Even if you have a half-hour to make your pitch, the first minutes should be devoted to whom, what and how the client is all about.

A good example of how to sell a product or concept can be found in the vacation timeshare industry. You know the drill. You're on vacation and are offered a free lunch, car rental or other incentive to tour a timeshare facility.

Having often attended such sales events, we have been struck by how the salesperson always starts by asking: What types of vacations do you like? Where do you go? How many times a year do you travel? Only after the sales person has gotten his targets thinking about vacations and such does he or she start to talk about the *benefits* of timesharing. The concept must work because timesharing has grown into a multi-billion dollar business.

At all times, focus on the needs of the small business buyer. Yes, we will admit that this is Basic Marketing 101 but it is often forgotten when small business leaders are the target.

## Objections and Questions Are Good Signs

Another factor we have seen in the small business space is dealing with objections and questions. Good salespeople view them as signs the prospect is interested. Poor salespeople view them as roadblocks. Robert Shapiro, a successful New York City commercial real estate broker, quotes a famous adage: "The sale begins when the customer says no." In all cases, your response and how you deal with them is important. As is the time needed to respond.

If a small business leader has a question, and you cannot answer it immediately, give them a time frame when you will have the answer for them… and stick to it!

If a small business leader is expecting an answer on a Monday morning, and it's now Tuesday afternoon and they still have not heard back from you, the odds of you selling them your products or services are "slim to none."

The study we talked about at the beginning of this chapter was conducted for a major corporation whose efforts to launch a product into the small business space had fallen flat. Among our tasks were to examine their materials and compare and contrast it with those of their competitors.

We found that three of the competitors were national brand name companies with long histories of selling to many markets. Their small business products ranged in price from $30 to $990 and were sold through telemarketing, online venues, through print advertising and via distributors. From this analysis and speaking with marketers within the industrial sector, there are some clear factors at work:

→ All marketers took their audience to be risk takers.
→ All marketers first emphasized their company and products, not the benefits.
→ None had really taken the time to explain their products' usefulness to their audience.
→ None offered a strong case for substituting their products for current applications.
→ None had demonstrated the ROI of substituting the new application for the old.
→ None used a small business leader as an endorser though one did have a Donald Trump-like celebrity.
→ There were no local components to the national marketing efforts although distributors were used.
→ The assumption was that one or two "touches" were enough to generate sales volume.

Unfortunately for these marketers and their customers this is not the best way to sell into the small business sector. Lest you think this was just one isolated case, the opposite is true. Over the years, we have seen this pattern repeat itself. Nor is it limited to specific industries or sectors. This is the antithesis of the *Janus Principle*.

This tendency becomes crystal clear at trade shows. Take a walk down any aisle. On both sides are booths for products and services intended to entice attendees to stop. The presumption you and I can make is that anyone exhibiting has spent thousands of dollars to create, ship, set-up and staff their booth.

Remember, attendees are walking these aisles to learn what is new; what products/services can be used by them; and how do they fit into their operations. Many attendees have appointments elsewhere and have limited time to spend on the floor. So how do exhibitors attract these potential customers?

Let's observe the signage above most booths. There is always the name of the company. In some booths, the product may be listed. In a few, quotes from people, trade press, national press and even an illustration can be seen. Nowhere is there a list of how it will benefit the passer-by.

How do these exhibitors expect attendees to stop? For many, the enticements are toys, gimmicks, contests, snacks, and pretty girls. Almost never do exhibitors highlight the benefits to attendees on the display spaces available.

Let's go inside the booth. We are greeted by staff members ranging from pretty secretaries brought to the show for decorative purposes or earnest sales people, male and female, who usually ask: "Have you heard of ABC Company? Or worse, "You have heard of ABC Corporation, we are the biggest supplier in the industry?" The visit goes down hill from there.

The most successful booth salesperson we ever saw was Rocky Piro, an old-timer who sold seeds for premium giveaways. Rocky's idea of an opening was to ask the visitor "What does your company do?" or "Why are you visiting this show and what do you need?" He told an audience at a sales meeting once that the key selling tactic he thought worked best for smaller companies was getting the person to tell you what he needed and finding a solution.

"My solution (packets of seeds) isn't glamorous or necessary, but I get them to look at the benefits their company will derive from handing out seeds instead of a fountain pen," he told anyone who would listen.

Rocky is now at that great trade show in the sky but what he said then applies even more so in today's world where personal contact is much rarer. Whether in person, via mail or through the Internet, the sales emphasis is inappropriately on the seller, not the buyer. Nowhere is that more true than in the Internet space.

Sadly, the Internet has produced a whole generation of younger marketers whose idea of salesmanship resides in giveaways, contests and drinking events. Our surveys of small business visitors to these exhibitions bear this out even more so.

In these convocations, we hear small business leaders complain that words and concepts are thrown at them without regard to what they need; how they are there to be educated and a feeling that they are being talked down to.

The assumption many of these booth personnel make is that they have the answer and the visitor need only listen to them to find their solution. The trouble is they never ask what the problem is. Visitors go to trade shows to find answers; it is up to the booth personnel to identify what are the questions and match their solution to the problem.

The Internet is another venue where we think selling the benefits first works well. In fact, we think it is a place where selling benefits first is the only way to market. However, judging by what we have seen, not too many marketers agree.

## The Importance of Follow-up

But let's go back to that walk down the trade show aisle. If you are like many attendees, you have left your information with various exhibitors. For many of us, it is safe to assume we will never hear from the exhibitor again. Indeed, in a study we did for a major show exhibition manager, the results astonished us. Fully 87% of leads from a sample group of 200 exhibitors were not followed up within three weeks of the show.

For Internet responses, the figure drops to 52% but a majority of that was a single email asking if the respondent wanted additional information.

When preparing this book, one of our authors went to a publishing show to identify a printer for the first galley copies of the book. In past shows, he had handed out his card after speaking with representatives about his general needs. At this show he spoke of specific need and deadline. Of seven potential vendors, only Starnet of Allandale, NJ. They got the contract.

Another example of how follow-up works well is found in the online insurance industry. There is a service called *Norvax*, which permits visitors to get their own quote on health and life insurance. Each agent or website sends their clients or visitor to a branded version of Norvax. If the visitor leaves his or her email, they receive a customized reply from the agent automatically. When Norvax provided a service that automatically sent seven additional emails over a spaced interval, sales went up an average 11%.

Repetition and follow-up works along with a good message. But the message is still the medium.

Keeping these thoughts in mind as one follows the *Janus Principle* is another key to successful small business marketing.

# Taking The Risk Out Of Marketing to Small Business Leaders

Risk has different meanings for organizations. Let's look at it from the *Janus Principle* perspective.

For a large organization, risk means putting at peril millions of dollars. It also means that there are guidelines in place as to how those funds are spent, what is expected in return and what managers must do to get them allocated.

Risk means something entirely different to the small business leader.

Every small business started out by someone taking a risk. Within the nation's poorer sections it often involved going "out-of-the-neighborhood" to obtain items in short supply. Returning, that entrepreneur then sold parts of his or her goods to neighbors. This kind of entrepreneurship still exists in many poorer sections of today's cities and rural towns.

In fact, there is a trend by some philanthropic organizations to organize micro-lending groups in under-developed countries. The *Small*

*Business Administration* (*SBA*) has tried to nurture this concept for years with mixed results. This has mainly focused on minority groups with loans as low as $7,500.

For more mainstream businesses, the situation often involves starting an enterprise from scratch and slowly building up sales and profits. Successful ventures have several things in common – persistence, hard work, an eye-on-the-bottom line and a willingness to trade effort for financial expenditure.

This sort of environment breeds a potential client who thinks three times before buying something new. He or she seeks out advice, often from friends or neighbors or other small enterprise leaders. What they won't do is take the word of someone they don't know.

Against this set of drivers, the marketer's organization puts up requirements that usually center on return-on-investment, sales progress, payback periods, and other financial considerations. In fact, most large organizational decisions are based on financial considerations and seldom on broader objectives. This is particularly true in products and services aimed at small business sectors.

There are few major initiatives aimed at the small business marketplace where losses are tolerated for long periods of time in order to gain market dominance. The *Janus Principle* now must be put in place to develop an approach that enables the successful marketer to gain the time necessary to gain acceptance.

Unfortunately, avenues open to marketers to help them build trust among small business leaders have severely declined. Once the main channel of many products for small business establishments were the local stationery stores. They acted as focal points for many products and services. The local stationery store leader was a member of the community and advised on many different aspects of business purchases. Unlike the large office supply chains, he or she knew the customer intimately and could advise based on more than the immediate need but on a long-term relationship.

The advent of *Staples* and *Office Depot* has driven many local stationary stores out of the market. While they have lowered the costs to small business leaders, they have also eliminated a significant advisor to the marketing mix. With the demise of this retailing sector, new sources of information and advice are needed. As we said earlier, *ISI* has found that the local independent drug store is now one of the last bastions of individual leadership with perceived wisdom. It has also found that these locations are filling the role of the local hardware, stationary, grocery and barbershop in dispensing purchasing advice.

Another impediment to building trust is the decline in customer service through reduced staffing at retail establishments. One result of today's retail environment everywhere is that many stores and shops are understaffed. What's more, those staffers who remain are not as knowledgeable as they once were and should be.

One only has to see the plight of *Home Depot* who, in a rush for greater profits substituted less experienced and knowledgeable floor workers and suffered a precipitous decline in sales. This was one of the contributing factors to the ousting of the company's CEO.

The fate of Robert Nardelli, this CEO, also reflects the differences when one fails in leading a big corporation and what happens to an entrepreneur. Nardelli was given *Chrysler Group* to lead into bankruptcy.. When an entrepreneur fails, he or she is left with debts and questions. Worse, his or her credit is often impaired.

*Ironically, if one were to look at this situation from a Janus Principle viewpoint, there is an interesting dichotomy. Large organizations that are risk adverse view the small business leader as a person who risks. Here is the Janus Principle working at its worst.*

Because they are innovators and risk takers in setting up their firms, small business leaders are considered risk takers. But ask any route sales person or distributor who has day-to-day contact with small business leaders and another picture emerges. That image is of a business leader who thinks three times before buying and uses a variety of sources to arrive at his or her buying decision. This trend collides with another fact of America in the 21$^{st}$ century.

In post-World War II America, distributors and route sales personnel fulfilled two important roles – sales person and deliverer of goods and services. Today, with mass distribution taking the place in many sectors of these functionaries, there is no intimate contact. For example, in the computer industry with the rise of the PC as a central feature of small business, VARs (Value Added Resellers) are the closest thing we have to those now-gone distributors.

Unfortunately, these VARs did not do the best job for small business leaders, particularly when broadband applications first appeared. They often overpriced and under-served their customers. The failure of Great Northern Telecom left hundreds of thousands of small business leaders without service and with hefty bills to pay. There is a saying, "once bitten, twice shy." For many business leaders the experience of broadband is still a warning to move carefully in today's technology world. That is why we argue that small business leaders as purchasing risk takers are a myth. Nowhere is the need to apply the *Janus Principle* more important than in this area.

In reality, the *Janus Principle* is roadmap by which organization can more fully focus their efforts on the small business marketplace and achieve maximum positive results. It essentially guides the marketing organization to look at the buyers within this sector through a prism that more fully highlights their buying process. By mirroring some of these activities, the organization can better understand the marketplace and focus on the key elements of the sales process that will motivate buyers.

These are the key elements of applying the *Janus Principle*:

- → Internalize the fact that there is a dichotomy between the way the organization operates and how small business leaders manage their enterprises.
- → Better understand the habits and motivation of small business leaders.
- → Adjust the company's marketing to the activities of small business leaders.
- → Create products/services that fit the needs of small enterprises and not expect small business leaders to adjust to the offerings.
- → Price the product/services to fit the small enterprise purchasing preferences within the parameters of the internal guidelines.
- → Be as flexible as the audience in the interaction between seller and buyer.

Most companies rely on market research to identify the needs and breath of a marketplace. This research often is reviewed in terms of the organizations internal bias. Few companies take the time or devote the effort to understand that there are fundamental differences in the operations of small enterprises versus their bigger brethren.

Equally as important, and, as we have stated before, smaller enterprises offering new products/services assume that because new is often better, small business leaders will purchase.

Internally, selling organizations understand the product/service, often use it themselves and feel little need to put themselves in the position of the buyer.

Selling organizations need to understand that there is a dichotomy that needs to be addressed when building and selling a product/service to this sector.

To start, let's remember that most small business marketing efforts fail because their proponents try to shoehorn a product or service aimed at one sector, usually larger corporations, into sectors with smaller enterprises.

Happily, we are seeing less of that these days, as lessons learned from past mistakes are sinking in with marketers.

What is true is that small business leaders need to feel that the product or service offering is designed with their operations in mind from the ground up. It is not enough to tell a business leader that the product worked well for a Fortune 1000 corporation.

What companies have failed to do is apply these concepts in many instances, resulting in less than successful products or services. One excellent example of this is the airline industry. While airlines fight to offer volume discounts to large clients, they utterly fail to provide the same services to smaller enterprises.

In surveys conducted on our travel site for small business, one-in-four respondents said they would be interested in seeking discounts from airlines in return for assured travel levels. They would also extend their patronage for vacation travel. Small business leaders tend to spend more on vacations in shorter bursts simply because they think they can't be away from their firms for longer periods.

Therefore, they would make excellent sources of extra income for airlines intent on filling seats. When we discussed this market sector with several airlines, their marketing people shrugged and said they could not devote the time based on the perceived sales volume.

Shortsighted? Yes, and, in the long run, self-defeating.

An airline marketer using the *Janus Principle* would evaluate, and in our opinion, find the rewards very profitable. They now think in terms of their business model requirements and not in terms of the selling possibilities, thereby leaving an untapped market unexploited.

Marketers to small business leaders have also not recognized the importance of providing superior support to smaller firms. One in six small business leaders surveyed by *ISI* and others say poor technical support was their biggest complaint. When asked what factors go into their decision to recommend a product to another company, one in three ranked support as the number one reason to withhold that recommendation.

Technical support often implies technology, specifically IT applications. But consider the case of a Connecticut located home-based business that went through three telephone suppliers in three months. Each promised superior service, on-time house calls and reduced costs. All three failed to deliver, in the meantime severely crippling the business. Will those firms get a recommendation or return business from this one enterprise? We doubt it.

Because larger organizations go through a multi-step process in purchasing, they often base their selling on the same principle. In contrast, smaller enterprises flatten the purchasing process.

Most small business respondents are not gatekeepers rather, they are the decision makers and they don't want to talk to a gatekeeper. By selling gatekeeper, we mean telephone solicitations, shotgun mailing programs and poorly thought out web tools.

To use *Dell* once more as an example, the company divides telephone response units by customer sector: consumer, small businesses and large corporate buyers.

Each is trained to service their particular sector and is a fully integrated unit. Even *Dell* does not do a totally effective job of managing the small business sector marketing but it comes very close.

If the marketing company doesn't have a telephone response mechanism they need more than a simple, all-things-to-all respondent kit.

For example, when someone requests information about the company's products or services, nothing beats a "personal letter" addressed to the person who made the request.

And while major corporations think all they have to do is "put their information on their website," and small business leaders will flock to them, it *does not* happen in the small business world.

In other words, big companies don't think like little company leaders, and that is their downfall. Make those follow-ups, keep it personal, and ask, and really mean, "How may we serve you?"

## Marketing Strategies That Work

No matter what the current economic enviroment there are marketing strategies to successfully market a product or service to small business. Even in a so-called "doom economy," small business marketing efforts can pay off.

## Key Appeals: Can I Make Money With Your Product or Service?

Another example of the *Janus Principle* is the differences in the primary motivation behind making a purchase between a large corporation and a small enterprise.

Large corporations purchase goods and services that are aimed at gaining more efficiencies. Small business leaders make purchases to increase sales or expand operations.

No matter how much time is allotted when creating the sales presentation for a small business leader, keep in mind they are always looking for ways they can make money and save money by using a product or service. So, the first big challenge is to convince them that they *will* make and/or save money by purchasing the product/service. They need to know "without a shadow of a doubt" that when they spend their hard earned money on the company's merchandise or services, they will not have a single regret.

It is amazing how many corporate sales campaigns fail to keep that "cash is king" mantra in mind as they attempt to tackle the small business world.

Small business leaders and executives will always be wondering what the return is on their investment? The key is demonstrating that the small business purchasers will obtain a significant return on their investment in a measurable time period. This time period needs to be relatively immediate and those results must play a part in their business success.

## Key Appeals: Need, Greed

The sales and marketing campaign or appeal has to reach one or both of these: Need and/or Greed. Keeping the "need and greed" scenario in mind when creating sales and marketing campaign will result in a higher success rate in the small business marketplace. Demonstrating a dollar and cents scenario is an excellent basis for any successful campaign.

Appeal to their **Need**: What will help them do their job better? What will help them do their job faster?

Appeal to their **Greed**: What will help them save money? What will help them make more money and/or fill a desire?

For many small business leaders, if you can sell them on the "need and/or greed" factor, you have made the sale!

## Summarizing What's Come Before

To this point, we have talked about the why, who, what, where and when of selling to small business leaders. Some of what we have said may appear elementary. Other parts counter-intuitive while some thoughts could be new to the reader and the company.

Our suggestions have all been tested in the marketplace at one time or the other and they consistently work. However, like everything else in business it is the execution that makes the difference. That is why we devote the remainder of this book to the "How" of adopting the *Janus Principle* and executing the company's efforts.

Bear in mind that is an axiom of war that "no plan survives first contact."

Therefore, it is important that the company adopt our suggestions to its own efforts and be prepared to be flexible in their execution but also remember that this process is a longer one than most executives realize.

We believe that adopting these tools and tactics to the company's efforts will lead to success in marketing.

## The How: Tools and Tactics

After having organized the company to better target customers, created the product/service to answer their needs, and developed an overall marketing strategy, the company is ready to employ the tools and tactics to make the sale.

To best leverage these efforts and before investing in marketing, it is necessary to develop an overall organizational content strategy. Whether in print, broadcast, online or out-of-office media, it is important for companies to speak with a consistent voice. An agreed upon organizational content strategy can ensure consistency, vibrancy and deliver value to customers. It is also effective in co-opting suppliers, employees, and others into the marketing process.

In reaching out to the small business leader, the company must make effective use of a multitude of delivery channels. The goal is to deliver at least seven "touches" to the small business leaders. On average, this is the required number needed to motivate him or her into purchasing a product/service.

These delivery channels include:

→ Print (includes trade press, national media, newspapers and books)
→ Online (includes websites, emails, microsites, blogs, texting, wikis, webcasts, podcasts)
→ Broadcast (includes radio, TV, cable, telephone)

We also mention a new marketing category consumer marketers use and small business sales teams are adopting – out-of-office channels, including transportation vehicles, transit points, hotels, and restaurants.

## Public Relations Efforts

Because in our experience public relations (PR) efforts have the best possible ROI of any single category (other than non-person-to-person), we will start the print section discussing how to apply the *Janus Principle* to this very effective tool.

Underpinning a company's efforts in all of these marketing areas should be an effective public relations campaign that drives content for both the print and online elements. Whether it is print, which is under severe financial pressure and is strongly in need of cheaper ways of obtaining editorial, or online venues with ever growing needs for content, providing that information is the most cost effective way of reaching small business readers.

One of the key reasons a company embarks on a public relations campaign is to gain credibility and traction with an audience.

No amount of advertising can beat a positive paragraph in *The Wall Street Journal* about a product or company.

No direct mail campaign matches in effectiveness a trade magazine's positive review of a new product for its readers.

No email campaign can generate the number of motivated visitors that a press release sent online can.

All of these venues are possible with an effective public relations campaign. But like everything else in life, good PR takes time, effort and common sense.

## Going Where Small Business Leaders Are

When asked why he robbed banks, Willie Sutton, the notorious bandit, replied: "Because that's where the money is."

The best way to reach out to the small business sector, as we have already pointed out on numerous occasions, is to "go where they are." In other words, move into "their world." And by that we mean read the trade publications that they read, listen to the radio stations that they listen to, and pay close attention to the public relations efforts of other companies that have successfully gone before you.

While spending a sufficient amount of money on advertising your product or service is very important, it is equally important to support that ad campaign with a carefully crafted PR plan of attack.

In our research, we have found that the average small business leader reads more than the population as a whole. He or she opens and scans at least three magazines each month and a newspaper at least every other day. This is twice or three times the national average.

Does that small business reader use the Internet? Yes.

Does he or she gather most of his or her information from that media? No.

Will trade and other media shift more of their efforts and information delivery to the Internet? Yes.

But for the foreseeable future, the base for these critical media will remain in more traditional channels.

Regardless of the media, print, online, or broadcast, in public relations efforts, the small business marketer has a powerful tool to build his or her product.

The advantages are three-fold:

- Appearance in a trade or national press implies the third-party endorsement critical to sales success.
- Dollar-for-dollar it has the most impact on the sales process.
- It gets your message across at a time when the small business leader is most attentive.

Obviously there are disadvantages to the public relation process:

- There is no control over what is said about your product.
- There is no control over when this material will appear or if it will.
- Public relation efforts take a long time to develop and fully impact the sales process.
- There are many PR practitioners but few good ones.
- The initial cost is high against the eventual payback.

➤ It requires a great deal of work on the part of the company.

Nonetheless, having good public relations is, in our view, one of the best ways of winning over small business leaders.

Having said that, let us give some suggestions about what and how to go about overseeing a successful public relations effort.

## Elements of a Successful PR Effort

Any successful PR effort starts by identifying the goals of such an effort. They include:

➤ Identifying the product, service or company that is to be highlighted.
➤ Defining who are your primary audiences.
➤ Creating a list of talking points about the highlighted product/service.
➤ Establishing who within the company is the spokesperson.
➤ Drawing up a list of industry outlets (print, online, radio, blogs).
➤ Finding the right PR person(s) to carry out the efforts.
➤ Allocating the funds for these efforts.
➤ Agreeing with the designated PR person on the goals and how they will be measured.
➤ Laying out the timeline for these efforts and staying the course.
➤ Executing.

Let's expand on these thoughts.

First, the company must agree on what it wants to publicize. The product and service is obvious, but equally as important, the company should figure in the public relation mix. It is easier for a large company to agree to this than a smaller, private firm. However, in both cases the reputation of the company must be built up along with the product.

Being a large corporation is not enough to sell a small business leader. We have in mind the famous incident described below.

In the early days of cable, *CBS* started the *Arts & Entertainment Channel* now known as *A&E*. They put a 52-year-old executive in charge and in his first interview with a leading trade magazine he was asked what the channel would be and why cable carriers should have it. His reply, "Because we're *CBS*," is now classic. Exit one president and enter years of struggle before success came to *A&E*.

The second step taken before PR counsel is sought involves identifying the audience for the product or service. The audiences can be defined by such characteristics as industry sector, size of company, small business leader, types of companies, users of particular software or equipment or any other dimension.

Usually, this is done as the product/service is being developed but sometimes there are primary and secondary potential users. Regardless of the dimensions used to segment, it is then easier to identify the media they read or use most frequently.

The talking points are also critically important. They should address the benefits of the product or service and include case studies. Words to be avoided are "best," "astonishing," "world-class." Words we suggest to be included are "proven," "designed for small businesses," "developed especially for small business," "advised by small business owners," and the like.

These talking points need to be concise, have credibility, and address the benefits of the product to the small business leader.

Naturally, these talking points should be discussed with the group charged with executing the campaign, but it helps them and the company if they are first created internally.

The company spokesperson will become the public face of the effort. This person must be personable, knowledgeable and willing to meet often with small business prospects. He or she will also be asked to make speeches and presentations at gatherings on a local level as well as within the sector.

The spokesperson should also have a bit of humility and ability to deal with all levels of the industry and society at large. This role is best suited for the company's president. However, too often we have seen this role shorted by the president. What's more, this individual, and all members of the company, should also be willing to listen to their PR counsel in matters of style, writing and the like to maximize the communication.

Defining the list of potential publications and media outlets is another area to be done prior to bringing on PR counsel. In PR, as in advertising, many companies favor national media at the expense of trade and regional publications. That is a mistake as they are often the final information source consulted by small business leaders.

This list can be obtained by talking with the company's sales force, as they are in direct contact with the potential users. There is a salesman of print supplies who regularly checks the waiting rooms of his clients to see what magazines they are reading. He identifies this brief survey as a snapshot of the industry and its current marketing channels. He also notes which person within the company the magazines are mailed to and often sees a hierarchy of purchasing by comparing the periodicals. One thing he always notes is that the most senior person in the companies that are most successful reads the trade books first, then passes them down the line.

As he often tells his boss, "I know who the final decision maker in each company is quickly."

The toughest part of the process is determining the PR counsel. Look for one that knows your industry, offering and target market. This will save time and increase ROI.

There are literally thousands of PR companies in the United States. The top 50, according to trade newsletters, control 85% of the "spend." In most cases, the largest corporations will opt for these large providers. Our experience, and those of our clients, indicates that a one or two-person operation can be just as effective. They are also cheaper and will devote more time to this effort while being very responsive to the client's needs.

The best way of finding out what fits the company's needs is to talk with each possible provider and be sure to check provided references. Sometimes, our clients have tested one or two PR groups with a defined project, perhaps helping in the launch of a new version or model line.

Regardless of the specifics of the counsel's size or staffing, there should be agreement on what are ultimately the goals of the project, the time set for its accomplishment, and who will be the internal source for all communications. A key element of success is that once hired, the PR counsel is sought out for advice and suggestions, and those proffered are taken.

Funds for PR need to be allocated and the budget adhered to. Often, companies will cut back if results are not seen immediately. This is a mistake because PR takes a significant amount of time to be truly effective.

In business, it is often said that patience has its own rewards, and that addage can be no more true than in PR. Media outlets need to be cultivated and stories prepared. Often, media outlets will not accept the first or second offerings from a new source. Trade publications will accept routine product announcements immediately, but user stories and other non-product related items take more time and persistance to find their mark.

Follow the PR counsel's advice and try to communicate new developments early enough that he or she can have the lead time to get them in print.

In our experience, a company should produce and distribute one press release every three weeks. They should each contain at least one user reference or experience. Every fourth release should be about the company and its efforts.

As we are writing this book, the "flavor-of-the-month" for PR is "stimulus spending." Companies aiming at the small business market should hold back on basing their entire program aimed at capturing these transitory dollars – whether it be directly or as part of ongoing promotional programs.

A PR campaign should have strategic as well as tactical goals with the individual components matched against the strategic goals.

The final results are really dependent on the execution. Execution is only as good as the joint-efforts of the company and the PR counsel. The counsel can only do as much as the company permits and devotes to the effort. PR is hard work and needs to be viewed as a long-term commitment with measurement often defined in terms of inches of copy or online mentions.

These are difficult to quantify but key to any marketing effort aimed at small business leaders.

Keep in mind, national media is important but local and trade magazines will drive sales.

Don't forget that newspapers, although, declining are still part of many small business leader's day. National syndicated small business columnists and local writers still play an important role in small business leaders' lives.

## Trade Publications

Let's talk about trade magazines in more detail. While the entire business-to-business print world is declining in ad revenue they are not doing so as major influencers to their audiences. This dichotomy is important to remember as many publications are shifting headlong on the Internet.

Whether print or online, these publications need content and that's where a good public relations campaign can significantly help market a product/service.

Are you reading the trade publications that small business leaders and managers are reading? If not, you are missing out on a golden opportunity to meet your target audience in a neutral environment.

Trade magazines succeed by teaching their readers how to add revenue and profits to their operations with industry-specific information and data. If the product/service being offered can do that, there is a natural "fit" of content provider (the provider) to the content user (the trade publication).

There is a delicate dance between the company and the publication, which a good PR counsel can orchestrate, if he or she has a cooperating client.

This minuet also applies to all the other media discussed in this section.

There are five rules we follow in producing trade oriented content:

➡ Keep the story to 450 words or less and have the publication ask for more.
➡ Make sure it is industry specific or specifies functional areas, wherever possible.
➡ Put the benefit in the first paragraph and don't start off with the name of the company and surround it with hyperbole.
➡ List three activities that the product/service can improve or supplant more cheaply.
➡ Have an example of an actual user wherever possible.

The contact number(s) should be to the PR counsel and one company representative. These phones should be manned and replies made promptly.

Press releases need to be sent out several ways. The most obvious are via the news wires – PR Newswire, PRWeb and the like.

Equally as important, the PR counsel should develop a list of trade publications with specific editor's names for the company's product or service.

Industry specific publications are those serving a specific niche such as florists, dry cleaners, lawn services, franchises, insurance agents, and the like.

Should the product/service not be industry specific but is rather a functional offering, more generalized trade publications can be targeted.

Here are some examples of trade magazines that are widely read by the small business community:

→ *BtoB Magazine:* Delivers timely editorials on all disciplines of business-to-business marketing.

→ *Business Insurance:* Is the trusted voice of the commercial insurance marketplace.

→ *ChannelPro:* Is the only industry magazine committed to providing targeted business and technology insights for IT channel professionals and consultants who work in the field.

→ *Consulting Magazine:* Is the industry source for the key decision makers and influencers in the profession to read about what's going on in that sector.

→ *COVER Magazine:* Delivers no-nonsense business news and feature stories, designed to improve the retailer's everyday business operations.

→ *Internet Retailer:* Provides practical and comprehensive information on the Internet's many applications in retailing, including web based promotions and marketing.

→ *Marketing At Retail:* Provides the tools that help branding professionals, marketers, agencies, and retail professionals successfully capture additional shelf space and trends.

→ *Origination News:* Is the largest publication servicing mortgage originators.

➤ *Smart Meetings:* Feature the latest in meeting industry trends, emerging technology, personality profiles, and updates on the best venues and locations.

➤ *Successful Promotions:* Shows you how effective imprinted promotional items can be for any kind of campaign.

➤ *Supply & Demand Chain Executive:* Provides comprehensive coverage highlighting business strategies trends and forecasts.

➤ *Target Marketing:* Covers all direct response media, including direct mail, telemarketing, space advertising, the Web and direct response TV.

These publications are listed only to provide the reader with a sampling of the more than 14,000 trade outlets available. In fact, small business leaders avidly read more obscure publications in their particular niche.

Learning what publications your customers read is still an important facet of marketing intelligence and should be on the "to do" list of a marketer.

## Other Venues

In addition to trade publications, the company should also have an article or two written about its products/services in newspapers, both local and in syndicated columns.

*Scripps-Howard,* the *Associated Press,* and other syndication services have columns devoted to the small business sector on what is essentially a daily basis. Making contact with their authors and providing information of value to small business readers can get the company a plug in hundreds of newspapers.

There is another wonderful source of public relations leads called *ProfNet* (www.profnet.prnewswire.com). This service allows reporters to ask for experts and information specific to a story he or she is working on at the time. Requests on this offering include speaker needs, product solicitations and other venues where the company's products can be highlighted. It is a very cost effective way of reaching small business leaders.

# Advertising

Often, when a press release appears, the company is approached by a sales person from the trade magazine to purchase an ad. This is standard operating procedure and should be viewed as an opportunity to explore advertising options.

Paid advertising is both an opportunity and pitfall for many marketers to small business leaders. The opportunity is that paid advertising gets the message across about the product or service. But because the small business marketplace is so diffuse and un-homogenized, reaching decision makers through advertising is that much more difficult.

For companies with industry specific products/services the task, in terms of advertising is less difficult. For companies with functional products/services the task becomes more complicated.

Many companies turn to advertising as the preferred method of reaching its target market. As this book is being written, business to business online advertising is gaining in total dollars while print promotion is nose-diving. We will discuss the online advertising in that section. For the moment, let's examine the print side of the advertising equation.

For industry specific products/services it is easier to identify possible advertising vehicles.

These are generally trade publications described above. No print ad today should be purchased without an online component, including webpage advertising, email blasts and online listings. This combo buying is becoming almost the norm within the industry and should be the company's position at all times.

One reminder: Make sure the message in the advertisements reflects the messages in the other components – press releases, trade show materials, etc.

For more functionally based products/services the task is more difficult. They need to cast a wider net to attract small business leaders from diverse industry groups and sectors.

The pitfall is that many marketers waste their money on the wrong publications.

## Placing Advertising

Based on the experiences of our clients, we have very definite ideas on where to place the company's advertising.

Given our choice between spending $100,000 on three pages in *Entrepreneur*, *Portfolio*, and *Inc.* versus six trade magazines, we would always choose the latter. Repetition is one reason, focus is the second and less clutter is the third.

If the company insists on having a presence in the former publications, then purchasing links on their websites are the recommended alternatives.

To summarize this section, we have found public relations efforts are an important element in successful small business marketing. Public relations are difficult and require the company to make adjustments as well as commitments to its success. Trade press is the key to print success in generating leads and sales. Newspapers and other mainstay media are still viable outlets. Advertising is an adjunct to this effort and not the driver.

We will now turn to another important media in the small business sector – direct mail.

## Direct Mail

In this section we will explore how to use off-line tools to sell products and services. In the next section, we will look at the online tools and tactics, as well as discussing social media, going viral, search engine optimization, driving conversion and RSS feeds.

Before we do, let's do some comparison and contrasts between the off-line tools (such as direct mail) and the online tools (emails and websites most particularly):

- → All marketing efforts have as their goal the sale.
- → How each marketing tool is used to accomplish this goal differ.

Direct mail and online efforts are usually aimed at getting the prospect talking to a sales person. This approach separates efforts into lead generation and direct sales.

In all the research we have done and others have completed, a good rule-of-thumb is that most small business leaders need seven "touches" to galvanize them into action.

Usually, these touches are done in combination – online, postal, telephone, sales person contact, and ultimately even executive-to-executive conversations.

Whatever the combination, all company efforts must be consistently espousing the agreed-upon theme.

The goal of every marketer is to minimize the dollars spent and maximize the dollars sold. To do this requires coordination and significant effort across many media fronts. We will try to give the reader an overview of all these channels with their applicability to the small business marketplace.

Not by accident will the majority of our efforts focus on direct mail and the Internet. However, the activities and suggestions we make will differ widely between the two media.

The former (direct mail) because it has and will continue to play a significant role in the marketing effort. The latter (email and websites) because it will play a much more significant role in the future.

The reader should keep in mind what Marshall McLuhan said: "the medium is the message."

For the marketer, the mantra is insuring that all content, no matter what the medium is consistent, informative, and generates sales.

## Postal Versus Internet

Let's first explore postal versus Internet, then move into specific practices and tactics for each delivery channel.

In today's small business marketing world, there are usually two major components to every campaign: alerting the target audience to what we do and how we do it.

The call to action drives them to the website but the real purchasing incentive message is usually contained in the postal mail. One reinforces the other.

Email gets out the message, promotes day-to-day efforts and creates a sense of belonging. It is also a two-edged sword as it sometimes gives out too much data without enough editorial context to permit better decision-making. It is a tactical weapon that needs a strategic overview as to its content and mission to be truly effective. One caveat, sometimes this approach substitutes in the firm's mind for personal contact, which can reduce the success factor in the long run.

## How Best To Use Postal Mail and The Internet

While email has sped communications, it has also cluttered the business day and night with the need for checking email more frequently and separating the wheat from the chaff. Whereas the once or twice a day postal mail runs made sorting information a limited activity, everyone now needs to do it four, five times a day for email and for those with PDAs it seems almost constant.

Email, if properly used, can reach the desk of a highly targeted company and/or small business leader at a time when their mind can be concentrated on this buy decision.

Probably the two most important attributes of email are its ability to reach precisely the target sought and allow for immediate reaction. Postal goes through several hands, not the least of which is the mailroom with its attendant possibility of misrouting or loss and getting through the gatekeeper assistant.

On the other hand, within the small business community, postal mail is still an effective tool for getting important, detailed information into the hands of intended targets. Email works for the broader message and attention getting; but postal is more effective in giving the reasons for acting, purchasing.

Depending too much on email can lead to misunderstandings and miscommunication of the company's goals and objectives. From a marketing standpoint, it leads to simplification of the message to the point where purchasing decisions become confused and delayed.

In the future, we believe that email and postal mail will work together more seamlessly and become more effective direct marketing tools.

## Advantages of Direct Mail

In the age of the Internet, direct postal mail still works.

Despite rising costs and other obstacles, for marketing to small business leaders it is a very effective tool.

There are many advantages to using a direct mail campaign to reach small business leaders, including:

**Selecting your target audience:** By using direct mail, you can target a specific audience to receive your advertising message. Are you looking for small business leaders who took out a loan to expand their company? Information like that is readily available.

**Holding your reader's attention:** By using direct mail, your ad does not have to compete with other ads on a newspaper page. Believe it or not, small business leaders can be persuaded to buy, if they get a compelling enough direct mail package.

**Getting rapid response from your prospects:** In most cases, a successful direct mail campaign can produce results in a fairly short time frame. Make sure you create a campaign that will convince or motivate them to respond.

**Using different strategies:** Because you have the ability to control your own mailing lists (and any mailing lists that you might rent), you can use different strategies to see what works best. For example, you can send one group of prospects a short letter, and another group a longer letter, and see which one works best and gives you the results you are looking for.

One thing you should know about small business leaders and direct marketing campaigns: depending upon how busy they are, and how much mail they receive each week, you may not get the immediate response you are hoping for. In other words, some small business leaders are so busy, they barely have time to open their regular mail, let alone spend time reading direct mail packages considered to be "junk mail."

## Plan The Envelope

One way to improve your chances of success is by having the right "look" to your envelope. Direct marketing experts agree that getting someone to open your mailing piece is half the battle. Then, once the envelope has been opened and they are scanning the contents, they have a few seconds before they decide to read it more in depth, or toss it away.

Above, we discussed the comparisons between postal and Internet (email) and the reader should re-read that section in relation to what we are about to discuss.

## Choose the Right Lists

If you are using any type of a direct mail or online marketing campaign to reach small business leaders, it is very important that you choose the right list. With the right list, you will make contacts that will lead to lots of sales. But with the wrong list, you will end up with too many dead ends. If you want your marketing campaign to succeed, do your homework when searching for a list.

Ask yourself these questions:

- **What type of list am I looking for?**
- **Can I guarantee the quality of the list?**
- **How well does the list I am considering match my target audience?**

Let's briefly look at each of the answers.

These days, usually there are lists available in one of three categories, including affiliation lists, response lists and compiled lists. Often times a compiled list will seem like the way to go; however, it is important to know that those lists are usually put together using information from public sources. In other words, the list may be big, but it will be filled with prospects that are probably not of interest to you. (In many cases, the compiled list will be nothing more than information culled from a telephone directory.)

If you rent a response list, you will get the names and contact information of people who have responded to a special offer, or perhaps purchased a particular product or service in the past. With this type of a list, you should have a higher rate of positive response, but that also means the price per thousand names will be higher than a compiled list.

Affiliation lists, also known as subscriber lists, may also cost more than compiled lists, and normally offer more bang for the buck. They are usually available with more detailed information than the other lists. For example, if you are searching for small business leaders who are members of the Chamber of Commerce, you will have success.

No matter what type of list you are looking for, make sure you ask about the quality. One important question to always ask is how old the contacts are. Some direct mail lists include people who are no longer interested in receiving offers, or even people who are no longer alive. Check references very carefully before purchasing any list.

## Have a Call To Action

In order for any direct marketing campaign to enjoy a successful run, there needs to be a call to action that provides an immediate response from the recipient. Think about the number of direct marketing pieces you have personally received over the past few years. Odds are, many of them were poorly written, confusing, and really did not motivate you to respond to their offer.

The challenge is to create a direct marketing piece that has a "wow!" factor. In other words, when the small business leader or manager reads it, they cannot wait to respond. Sometimes that can be accomplished in the first few sentences; other times, however, it may take a page or two of compelling sales copy to seal the deal.

It is important to remember that the people on your target list may not be familiar with your company and the products or services you are trying to offer. So, create the best first impression and knock them off their feet. A poorly written direct mail piece gives the wrong impression about you and your company, but a well-written piece can translate into sales.

# Guidelines For Creating Direct Mail Campaigns

While no one can guarantee success in every direct mail campaign, there are some things you can do to improve your chances of success, including:

➤ Design the mail piece so the small business leaders see and understand what the most important benefit to them will be, either in a large headline, or the opening paragraph.

➤ Repeat your offer at least three times. Just like a radio commercial where people need to hear the name of your business several times, readers also need to read your offer/information at least three times.

➤ Use a friendly, easy to read conversational tone in the sales copy.

➤ Do not forget to use the buzzwords that are sure to catch the reader's eye: *free, save, profit, improve.*

➤ Remember to use lots of short paragraphs. Your letter can be a long one, but break up the paragraphs so the reader's eye doesn't panic at the thought of reading too much.

➤ Provide contact information (telephone number, email, mailing address) so the reader can easily follow-up; plus this adds credibility.

➤ When including the "response vehicle," be creative. Use a coupon, a postcard, letter that can be used to return for further information, or to take advantage of a special offer.

➤ Set up a special page on the company's website geared to the campaign and provide additional information and incentives to visitors.

➤ Include testimonials and quotes; they can be very convincing.

➤ Whenever possible have the name of a small business leader on the envelope and letter. Never address the direct mail package to "business leader." If you do, it may end up in the trashcan.

➤ Add a postscript (P.S.) at the end of the letter. Studies have shown that people will sometimes skip portions of a direct mail letter, but will be drawn to the P.S. Therefore, you should use that P.S. to your advantage, and hopefully, that will entice them to read the rest of the letter.

As we were writing this book, our company received a direct mail piece that talked about a new telephone service that would enable someone to take our calls and turn them into sales leads. All very good but the piece did not state until page three that by doing this, our company would increase overall sales by 35% or more or the company would give us our money back.

As the noted direct marketing Guru Roger Bly says, "The key is to *sell the benefit* first."

While in a large corporation it is always safe to "buy IBM," the small business leaders react better to the "benefit" sell. In other words, the small business leader has to understand and believe what the benefit will be before they will even consider making a purchase.

In direct mail, it is best to sell the benefits up front. Explain those in easy to understand language, and you have your foot in the door, and will most likely make that sale.

Many credit card companies bombard small business leaders with offers of business credit cards. "Sign with us, and we'll give you $25,000 worth of credit." That seems to be their "big selling point." However, just imagine the headline reading something like "We have the answer to your cash flow issues: a line of credit using our credit card!"

Every small business needs cash, especially for unexpected emergencies that seem to develop at the wrong time. Sell the benefit: in this case, the "peace of mind" that the small business leader will receive from signing with your credit card company and you will have a "win-win" scenario. And, when the small business leader is happy, again, they will tell their friends and business associates.

Many credit card companies utilize a fictitious "Vice President of Marketing" on their direct mail pieces. They have found that it increases response rates by 1-2%.

When using a name or title, if there is a phone number to call, the respondent should be reaching an American operator.

Unfortunately, when a caller responds, they are usually sent to an operator in India. In many instances, these call centers have specific answers to specific questions in a script and can't go beyond these parameters.

Often, the small business leader has other specific questions, which can't be answered through a scripted program.

Part of every good direct mail campaign is having someone ready and able to answer questions. This is another part of the equation that we will talk about later.

## Using the Right Direct Mail Service Provider

If you do not have the resources in-house to create a direct mail package, you should consider hiring a professional provider to do it for you. Direct mail specialists come in many different varieties, so choose one wisely. Look in the Yellow Pages, read direct mail trade publications and start looking. Collect information and ask for references before making a final decision.

Articulate what you are looking for, and make sure you are comfortable with what they can provide. Their specialists should be able to create the entire package, or you can assemble a direct marketing team yourself, doing some work in-house, and hiring out the other parts.

The team consists of the following:

→ The creative contributors: This includes both the artwork and the writing of the sell copy. The creative contributors can be instrumental in putting together a campaign that works well.

→ The list developers: They are in charge of assembling names, addresses and other contact info for your target list. The more research you devote to creating the right list, the higher success rate you will achieve with your direct mail package.

→ The printer and the mailing house: Don't scrimp when it comes to printing; a cheap looking direct mail package sends the wrong message about your company. The mailing house will ensure that your direct mail package meets all postal rules and regulations.

## Tips on Creating the Direct Mail Package

Direct mail letters are judged by one criterion: How effective are they? Grammatical perfection, brevity, a dignified tone are not necessarily attributes of successful direct mail letters.

One direct mail letter will not do it all. The letter written for prospects is very different from the one written for existing small business clients who know about the company and are satisfied customers. The goal with prospects is to gain their interest and support.

There are some basic rules for writing a good direct mail letter. They must always:

→ Interest the reader within the first paragraph.
→ Present information in a way that holds interest.
→ Present enough information to make the case.
→ Clearly state the benefits to the small business leader – the more specific the better.
→ Motivate the reader to take action.

The style of the direct mail letter involves:

→ Tone: Many direct mail letters are boring. The tone of direct mail pieces should imply a positive opportunity for small business leaders that will fill a basic need (solve a problem or help them operate their business at a more efficient level) or satisfy a want/desire (grow sales or expand geographically).
→ Flow: Ideas should flow from one to another in the right order of logic and interest.
→ Suspense: The letter should be too interesting to put down.
→ Personality: Even if a letter is ghostwritten, the signer should edit in some of his or her own style.
→ Language: It should be personal, hard-hitting and dramatic. Phrases like these are tried and proven effective, they include:
  *"And in just a moment I'll tell you how…"*
  *"And that's where you come in…"*
  *"My pledge to you is this…"*
  *"If you haven't yet decided whether to join us, let me…"*

The format of the letter should:

→ Create interest.

- State the problem.
- Arouse emotion.
- Offer hope for a solution.
- Allow the reader to participate in solving the problem.
- Induce action.
- Thank the reader for acting.

If the first paragraph doesn't interest the reader, the letter is a failure. Too often, the initial effort by any writer results in the best lead being buried three paragraphs down. After the writer drafts the letter, someone should look back through it and perhaps find a more winning opening for creating interest.

The letter should be long enough to present a compelling case. In the past brevity was the norm but four to six pages are becoming common. The challenge is to sustain interest and get the reader to act.

One of the best copy writers we know, John Rafferty, believes that the editorial should build in such a way that the target reader sees the benefit first, identifies the company's offering as the solution and is moved to action.

Underlining, handwritten margin notations, parentheses, bullets, italics and boldfaces are often used to draw the reader's attention to key points. However, the letter shouldn't be embellished to the point of confusion or illegibility.

The "P.S." is also very important. It is the last chance to drive home the most important point and urge the reader to take action.

## Content and Cleaning

Even when marketers use highly personalized letters that begin "Dear James" and end with a signature the results get muddied when "James" receives five different letters, identical with the exception that one is "Dear Jim," another "Dear J," etc.

Another problem is when direct mail marketers continue to send missives to employees who have left the company. Worse, if the employee has died. One home-based company receives mail for the man's divorced wife, six years after the parting.

Remember, small businesses are highly personalized and something like this indicates you really don't know or care about their firm or needs.

Direct mail campaigns need to be clear, repetitive and have a call to action, as well as provide a telephone number, website and mailing address for queries and questions.

## More On Content

The written word is a powerful tool and when correctly executed can be an effective means of establishing the company in the hearts and minds of potential small business customers. This applies to both off-line and online efforts. Many efforts are sabotaged by incorrect notions of what good business-to-small-business copywriting should be.

Here are *the most common and destructive myths* that undermine the impact of copy efforts in many cases:

## Don't Be Negative

The old song phrase, "accentuate the positive" applies to business copy of any sort. Saying something destructive about competitors, the company or small business customers is counter-productive.

*But, there are exceptions!*

Fear is every bit as powerful a motivator as desire, and when the situation is appropriate it makes perfectly good sense to communicate the negative consequences of not taking action or not buying your product.

Highlighting rising costs, safety hazards, failing health, lost opportunities, any of these "negative" issues can be effective motivators. As we write this book, recession fears are rampant across the country. Small businesses are particularly vulnerable in a down cycle because they have less available resources to wait out the downturn.

Offering solutions to these fears will gain the attention of any small business leaders. If the product/service can alleviate this concern, the communication vehicle should shout it throughout the copy. Just be certain the prospect isn't left dangling in fear, and position the offer as the release from the tension, the solution to the problem.

## Appeal To The Emotion, Not The Intellect

It has been argued that consumer copy speaks to the emotions, business copy to the intellect. The truth is consumers and business folk are the same people, just in different roles; people don't leave their feelings at home when they go to work.

To put this in perspective, consider the way key decisions are made in the company. Some are carefully considered, rational analysis while others are spurred by the hope to succeed, a fear of failure, a desire for recognition and reluctance to be humiliated. Selling to small business leaders is every bit as emotional as motivating consumers. The efforts speak to a different set of emotions.

To create effective impact, the copy needs to target the right emotions and varies depending on the nature of your offer and industry. Appealing to emotions also creates a sense of urgency and not targeting the right emotions reduces the impact and effectiveness.

Repetition is another consideration in creating effective copy, particularly in online efforts where repetition still plays a key role. Radio editors follow the dictum: "Tell them what you will say. Say it. Then tell them what you said."

For direct mail and online efforts, it is a good rule to follow.

## Direct Mail Timing

There is an old saying: "Timing is everything."

When you mail to your list it is also important.

If the company's target industrial sector has a busy time, try to "drop" the mailing ahead of this season. For instance, retailers have their busiest times before Christmas. They are usually spent by the time January rolls around so February is a better month to send them new ideas or product offerings.

Direct mail often can't show a direct correlation between being seen and making a purchase. The guideline, as we have said, is that a small business leader needs seven "touches" to promote an act.

Marketers often think only in terms of publications when thinking about print. To reach small business readers with print based products at a high ROI it is necessary to think outside the box.

We have a friend, Artie Parillo, who has come up with a novel way of reaching small business leaders. He contracts with pizza stores to deliver their products in pre-printed boxes to sell business insurance. Parillo provides the pizza shop with two types of pre-printed boxes, one designed for consumers at home and the other for delivery to business establishment.

Parillo started in North Jersey and is gradually moving west. His message to advertisers is simple: "I am delivering your message to an office or factory at a time when it will be read."

We conducted two studies, when we heard about Parillo's approach. Sure enough, the message was seen, discussed, and, more importantly, acted upon.

This print venue mimics one of the oldest direct mail offerings available – the card deck. This is another high ROI approach whereas a consolidator takes a number of advertisers, puts them in a cellophane envelope and sends them to a selected, agreed upon audience.

The hit rate for these is low but then again so is the cost. The result is a very high quality lead.

It is our experience that this type of marketing is going away but in a recent survey of 10,000 business leaders, we found that they opened these cards because they were often a novelty rather than an everyday occurrence.

Marketing professionals are also honing on a new concept – transpromotion.

Does this work? The approach was used by several credit unions launching their Health Savings Account (HSA) programs. They put the announcement of this new offering in the monthly statement envelopes sent to members. Several had a 22% response rate from their business clients during the first three months by using an insert in the statements sent to business and members.

Most of us who have credit cards see this approach every month.

Applying it to the invoices and mailings to clients can speed the sales cycle. After all, these clients already know about the company.

Exchanging inserts with non-competitors can also expand the marketing effort.

Case studies give prospects insights into how the company can help them overcome their fear of making the wrong decision. As we discussed earlier, this is fundamental to understanding the marketplace. Fear of making the wrong decision is a primary motivator in the small business supplier selection process. By demonstrating through actual examples, including testimonials and detailed case studies, how the product/service has helped another company, trust in that offering can be built.

As we are writing this book, *Verizon* is conducting such a campaign using both direct mail and emails to deliver case histories to small business leaders. While the jury is still out, we see significant click-throughs from small business leaders in our program with Verizon.

The case study can't just tout results; it should be made available either in print or online in story form. Telling the audience about a product/service, how it is being used and the results is one of the best ways of getting your message across.

However, if you're going to give valuable information about proprietary processes and how those results were achieved, post an abstract of the case study publicly and require registration to get the details and related pertinent information.

The distribution process is discussed in more detail in the online section with White Papers, where electronic copies of case studies are embedded with links to relevant pages on the company site. Case studies should be available in printed form for sales people to use and for distribution when information is requested.

Mail only distribution is almost a thing of the past but it still has its role in the small business marketing effort.

## Literature Requests

Many companies think of literature requests as expensive and passé. Many more consider them necessary but less effective parts of the sell process. Most salespeople want literature when they visit a client or respond to a request for information.

Printed material denotes to the recipient that the company has substance and credibility. Readers know that electronic marketing can be cheaply created overnight. In our surveys, we have found that small business leaders like to have printed material to review when making a buying decision. What's more they keep the material and pull it out to refer to, especially if things go wrong.

One manufacturer we know has catalogs and specification sheets going back to 1957. His collection should be donated to a museum if for no other reason than to see the changes in graphics and emphasis over the years.

One caveat, if your company offers print literature, then provide a mechanism for website visitors who request information to get it quickly. Nothing is more disastrous to the sell process than having material show up four, six or even eight weeks after being requested.

As we pointed out in the section on trade show marketing, promptness and follow-up are keys to effective small business marketing. These keys apply to print material distribution as well.

The examples above give the reader an idea how reaching small business leaders effectively can often mean looking at every day activities and finding ways of getting the company's sell message to them.

This is the *Janus Principle* working again. Look inside the company for ways that it interacts with clients and customers and find avenues to reach them with the sell message.

## Online Marketing

Nothing has changed the business world like the Internet.

From novelty to absolute requirement, the Internet is the channel of choice for much of our communications today.

Like every new idea, the Internet has spawned new methodologies as well as hyperbole. There are more gurus than there are stars in the sky. All of them talk about the Internet as a mystical place with rules and requirements that are often arcane and unique.

We have been using the Internet almost from its commercial beginning. As chairmen of an Internet audience aggregation company in early 1994, we helped bring it to an IPO in the halcyon days of the first boom.

From that first experience, we have noted many changes – good and bad.

What we have noted of late is that companies are starting to realize that they must utilize the Internet as an integral part of an over-all campaign. It is not by accident that advertising agencies, as this book is being written, are integrating their staffs so that the Internet is another function of the advertising offerings and not housed in separate companies.

At the same time, companies are starting to merge the various marketing components so that they can better coordinate their marketing efforts.

An effective online strategy involves coordinating the website, emails, blogs, and other Internet components with a response program that makes them doubly effective.

Our experience in building a marketing channel of more than five million responsive readers, the majority small business leaders, has shown us many lessons. This experience has also demonstrated that the time and effort required to be truly effective is far more than originally postulated by the Internet gurus.

What follows are our suggestions on how to reach small business readers via the Internet. Again, we base these suggestions on the *Janus Principle*, which encourages companies to look inside at their own operations and to apply the common sense lessons to their online offerings.

## Emails

Emails are the best and worse of Internet marketing. At their best, they are an affordable way of reaching highly targeted audiences at low expense; and at their worst, they create negative feelings and feedback when they become an annoyance.

The number of emails sent and received is growing exponentially. In fact, one may argue that getting a message through in this age of spamming (when +85% of messages sent are unsolicited) is becoming more difficult each day.

Many of us wonder what we did before the advent of email. As we write this book, some critics are even saying that emails are passé. Nonetheless, emails clutter everyone's in box. One study indicated the average business executive (in large and small organizations) spends up to two hours each day checking email. Much of this effort is separating the important from the less important and junk mail. As we said earlier, where once or twice a day postal mail runs made sorting information a limited activity, we now need to do it four, five times a day for email and those with PDAs it seems almost constant.

We have seen this medium grow from novelty to a vital force in today's economy. At the same time, we have also seen successful efforts and those that have failed miserably. There are certain conclusions we can draw from all of these experiences. They include that:

→ **New media need different ideas but some of the old rules still apply.**
→ **The personal touch is still needed.**
→ **Multiple online messages are needed to seal the deal.**
→ **Brick sites still help in selling online.**
→ **Brevity beats verbosity.**
→ **Patience still has its rewards.**
→ **Generational differences abound.**

On the Internet, there are few rules and fewer barriers to entry. At the same time, small business leaders are still learning to adapt to this medium as a sales, information and purchasing channel.

Most small business leaders still use it only as an information-gathering tool and rely on other influencers to make their decisions. We believe that this will change over time but emailing will still be part of the process, not the end-all.

Nonetheless, many corporations view the Internet as a cost-effective channel to reach small business leaders. We agree. As an advertising vehicle, if properly used, it can reach the desk of a highly targeted function, i.e. CIO, purchasing agent, or CFO.

Does the company rely heavily on marketing its product or service on the Internet? That might work well if the target audience is used to just visiting the website, reading about the product or service, and clicking through to the ordering page.

However, that technique and marketing strategy will not work with a small business leader. They will not act on the Internet until they see something at least seven times. Again that seven touches rule is in play.

On the Internet, there are few rules and fewer barriers to entry. At the same time, small business leaders are still learning to adapt to this media as both a sales and purchasing channel.

The one barrier that is growing each day is spamming.

Everyone gets spam, and it's unbelievably annoying. It's gotten so bad that a federal law was passed in an attempt to rein it in.

THE FCC'S CAN-SPAM RULES

The FCC's ban on sending unwanted e-mail messages to wireless devices applies to all "commercial messages." The CAN-SPAM Act defines commercial messages as those for which the primary purpose is to advertise or promote a commercial product or service. The FCC's ban does not cover "transactional or relationship" messages, or notices to facilitate a transaction you have already agreed to. These messages would include statements about an existing account or warranty information about a product you've purchased. The FCC's ban also does not cover non-commercial messages, such as messages about candidates for public office.

However, as an effective marketing tool to inform and motivate, email works.

There are few secrets to emailing that can't be learned quickly on your own. In the small business marketplace, they consist of:

➤ Having the right list.
➤ Crafting an effective subject line.
➤ Providing actionable information.
➤ Creating an effective call-to-action.

→ Posting a landing page that invites readership.
→ Following up on all leads immediately.
→ Posting fresh material on a regular basis.
→ Sending additional emails on a regular schedule.

The first requirement is a good list. We usually tell our clients to build their list internally first. If companies looked at their own communications with clients and prospects, the basic list can be created almost immediately.

For some of our clients, we have devised ways of getting around some of the restrictions and hurdles associated with sending out emails.

To comply with CAN-SPAM, we suggest that they create a White Paper about an important aspect of the offerings. This White Paper should address a concern of their clients. One company we advised that provided software for small business owners to complete their taxes created a White Paper on the ten most glaring examples of deductions not taken by companies in filing their returns. Another offered a list of potential marketing venues that companies could use to sell products.

When individuals downloaded these White Papers, they were asked to opt-in for more information. The average opt-in in some cases was over 50%.

With these as starters, these companies then went out and bought lists to offer them to new, potential clients. The sign-up rate was above 20% of those that opened the email.

Many companies have corporate policies against sending to anything but opt-in lists. One company we know requires that any list it purchases must be specifically qualified to receive their emails.

While this is an extreme case, companies are sensitive to spamming rules. That does not mean that non-opt-in lists cannot be used.

To be on the safe side, turn to reputable list brokers such as *Merit Direct, ALC, DirectInnovations* and *L-I-S-T*.

There is another important element to list selection. Choosing a list which requires making decisions based on costs and quality.

Compiled lists are those offered by many large data houses and are just that – compiled data from a variety of sources.

Reader lists are those offerings that are drawn from readers of publications either print or online. Our 5+ million record list is made up of readers of our newsletters. Publishers such as *Penton, Business Week* and others also offer lists made up of their readers.

We think the higher the quality of the offering, the higher the quality of the list chosen. That quality should extend to the copy, presentation and landing page.

We have built our lists on providing good content, which is the key to success on the Internet. Therefore, it is a high quality list as are many others on the market. This quality comes at a price. These lists often cost more and are usually not open to everyone. Many also require that they approve the content of the email being sent.

But before we talk about content, let's look at the subject line, which we feel is the most important of the campaign elements. The subject line is like the envelope on a direct mail piece. If it gets the interest of the recipient, he or she will open the email. If not, it goes into the trash folder.

The subject line must be compelling, succinct and relevant. It needs to be viewed as the equivalent of a newspaper headline. If the headline doesn't grab the reader, the rest won't be even looked at.

Over the years, we have tested many subject lines and approaches. Among the things we have learned are:

➜ While "free" is a great direct mail postal word it seems to raise warnings on spam filters that block many messages with it in the subject line.
➜ Highlighting a negative, such as *10 Most Common IRS Filing Errors,* to small business owners seems to increase their open rate.
➜ Addressing a need with a solution works well.
➜ Fewer words lead to a higher the open rate.
➜ Emotional words garner attention.
➜ Who the email is from is almost as important as the subject line words.
➜ Offering something of value in the subject line works well.

The best subject line we have seen in recent years came from *WellPoint Insurance.* The company was offering healthcare insurance to small business owners in several states. In the subject line, WellPoint offered a report on reducing healthcare costs. Reducing healthcare costs is a major concern of small business leaders. The subject line highlighted a concern and offered information on easing that concern.

While it varied somewhat, the major subject line was: "*Special Report: Reduce your healthcare costs.*"

This subject line had a 28% open rate and 8% click-through to their landing page.

Open rates are often discussed in the context of emailing. The same group faced with differing subject lines will have varying open rates. We think that anything over 20% is good for the small business marketplace.

Other authorities have differing numbers, but we view this as the threshold for good emailing.

The subject line should not set off spam filters. You can test this by sending the email message to yourself at your company while your spam filters are turned on. You have to send it from outside the company to ensure that it passes through the company filters.

After the subject line, content is important.

Preferably, a good email offers the recipient an incentive that is of perceived value. Examples are White Papers, free trial software, coupons, special offers, free articles, free merchandise upgrades or contests.

The copy needs to be short and succinct and written in a conversational tone. It shouldn't be more than a few small paragraphs and require no scrolling to read the key sell points.

The copy should talk about what the product/service can do for the recipient (don't talk about yourself or your company – no one cares).

Ideally, the email should be personalized, as in "Dear Jack." Personalized emails tend to have a 10% better click-through rate than non-personalized offerings. WellPoint personalized their offering in one state and the click-through rates went up 10%.

There ought to be only one call to action. In other words, there should be only one hyperlink in the email message that brings the recipient to a page on your website that offers the incentive, first requiring that recipients fill out a short HTML form before they can get the incentive. The hyperlink should be repeated through the copy to maximize clickthroughs.

Collecting names and email addresses has become the norm on

websites; and the majority of users are willing to give out business contact information to receive an individualized online experience. However, asking for an email address will cut down on the number of visitors who will download the offering.

The company should decide what is more important – getting out the message or collecting names.

Emailing is about generating leads. One of the most important aspects of gaining leads is the landing page to which you send your email recipients.

When advertisers seek to use our list of 5+million subscribers, we urge them to create a landing page that tells the visitor what are the benefits of the product/service offering in the first 25 words. Unfortunately, most marketers create pretty websites that talk about the company, the people and perhaps, finally, the product before presenting the benefits.

Let's give you two examples from our own experience.

In one, an Atlanta company with a dynamite product that reduces the need for individuals to purchase or download special equipment to see their televised web seminars teamed with us to sell the service.

More than 1,000 business leaders clicked through to their landing page without a single person asking for a demo.

The landing page met all of our suggested criteria but still failed. In this case, we identified the problem. We pushed the benefits but failed to realize that they were the wrong benefits.

When we surveyed the audience, we found that their need was a way of reaching their representatives, not their clients.

In the second example, a 2.0 vendor of services to help build the firm's image bigger than it was by installing a suite of communications tools. The secret of its success; the new client changed nothing, not even its phone number, but simply signed on for the service. The offering could be disconnected in minutes and the contract was on a month-to-month basis. What is the catch? There was a free one-month trial. Results: 457 click-throughs and 25 sign-ups.

As we have stated earlier, there are always two components to every campaign. Alerting the target audience to what we do and how we do it. The call to action  drives them to the website but the real purchasing incentive is contained in the postal mail. One medium (direct mail) reinforces the other (email) and vice versa.

Email gets out the message, alerts staff, promotes day-to-day efforts and creates a sense of belonging. It is also a two-edge sword as it sometimes gives out too much data without enough contexts to permit better decision-making on the part of the recipient. Better decision-making is really another phase for making the sale.

Emailing is a tactical weapon that needs strategic overview to be truly effective. Sometimes, it substitutes for personal contact, which is rapidly becoming a problem for many companies. At its worse, email cuts the human contact and is perhaps most personified in the use of emails to fire people that we are hearing about more and more.

One activity often overlooked in the emailing process is the follow-up. Like the trade show vendor, many companies do not follow-up on the leads generated.

In our experience, fewer than 10% of all click-through visitors who leave an email address get effective follow-up.

This wastage is a key factor in the low ROI expected of an email campaign. Every email campaign should have at least three follow-up components to reach visitors.

It is elementary but still happening too often.

To sum up the email process, we offer the following four implementation steps to online email marketing, they include:

➤ 1. Identify: Build a house list. Develop a qualification system – A leads (hottest, biggest), B leads (hot, big), C leads (good), and D leads (requires follow-up) - and be sure to qualify each lead you get.

➤ 2. Differentiate: Determine the significant differences among the list of people. For example, by prospective customers and existing customers, by title, by geographical area, or by product interest, just to name a few.

➤ 3. Interact: Establish a dialog with your prospective and existing customers. Engage them using anticipated, relevant and personal emails.

➤ 4. Customize: Tailor your marketing messages, your subsequent emails in this case, based on what has been learned during the previous interactions. Each message or "conversation" will be different, based on the specific preferences.

## The Website

Increasingly, the company's website is the front door to the establishment. Like any front door, how it appears to the visitor makes an important impression. Often it is the only impression that visitor will have.

In our analysis of small business leader Internet usage we found that 87% never got past the first (index or home) page on their initial visit.

Stop and think about it.

A significant majority of small business leaders come to the company's front door and don't step in. There are many reasons for this but often the simplest explanations are the most compelling.

For another client, Access Insurance, we provided advice and counsel on marketing their insurance services to smaller businesses. We created the website and tweaked it over a year.

There were several things that improved usage and got visitors past the front door.

Perhaps the simplest was that we made the type more readable. The copy stayed the same but we separated the paragraphs and increased the type font by one size. The result, average page per visit doubled with just that one change.

Another change was adding a "Who we are" section.

In our studies, this page was viewed by 34% of all first time small business visitors. This is an astonishing number and means that this page is a critical element in their decision to do business with the company.

Many firms put their information on the front page, usually with hyperbola. Carefully presenting the company on the "Who we are" page is a better solution. It is both a sell-point and an indication that the visitor is interested. This page should also have information on contacting the company and not, as most website do, a separate section, or just an online email form. Whoever is designated to answer the phone or email should be monitoring this daily with weekend coverage.

If the company's doorway (the index page) is the only thing they see on the first visit, what are some of the key elements that should be on this pivotal page?

Our research and that of others indicate that small business leaders do much more research than consumers and large corporate buyers as part of the buying process.

The company's ability to establish confidence and credibility by writing intelligently and persuasively about its product/service becomes critical to long-term success.

Content after initially emphasizing that the company can provide a solution to the visitor's need, should then clearly articulate the selling propositions – how it satisfies the visitor's needs.

If a landing page is used for an email blast, it should be separate from the first (index or home) page and specifically address the solution to the problem articulated in the email. And it should do this in the first 25 words or less that the visitor reads.

The website's entire personality will significantly impact whether the company will continue to be considered as a potential supplier. Therefore, not only the landing page copy needs to be compelling so does copy on every other page.

What then does a company do with its website to make it so appealing that the small business leader will open the door.

There are many differing views on what an Internet index page should look like. Our suggestions will only apply to small business leaders and their feedback to us.

These suggestions focus more on the content rather than the design as that is an area that has many viewpoints. However, it is the words and what they say to the visitor that are the focus of our suggestions.

Here are a few suggestions to make your company website more successful with the small business user:

Focus on information architecture rather than design. Concentrate more of your company's budget on the proper website "blueprint" and then layer on a nice design.

Research the elements that are very specific to your target audience.

Remember that website usability and search engine optimization go hand in hand, and more than 90% of the time, work with each other.

Most companies try to make their websites all things to all people. That is the first mistake. We have examined over 500 websites aimed in part at small business leaders. Often, these websites are designed to serve multiple audiences, asking them to choose the door to their particular needs. This is self-defeating as it requires the visitor to make an additional "click" before reaching his or her specific page.

We always suggest to our clients that they create a special portal just for the small business visitor. *American Express* differentiates its products with separate websites and drives traffic accordingly. While many companies don't have *American Express'* marketing budgets, they can separate by size category.

This means that if ACME Corporation has multiple target audiences, it can have the corporate website as well as those for its small business products/services.

Whether it is the first click for small business visitors or an individualized website the first page should have four basic elements:

➤ Copy that talks to the needs of the visitor.
➤ An easy to use navigation protocol that invites the visitor.
➤ Graphics that reinforce the company message.
➤ Leaders to encourage exploration.

Let's look at these elements one at a time.

Our suggestions about content fall into three categories – the first 25 words, the navigation scheme and call to action.

The first 25 words read upper left to lower right are the key to opening the door. Studies show that visitors are focused on those opening words or dominant elements.

The first or most prominent elements should speak to how the company will help the visitor. For instance:

"Widgets reduce strain on clipper ship masts enabling them to carry fuller sails."

"Acme widgets last twice as long, cost 30% less than most competitors."

These 25 words tell the benefits to the visitor of ACME's offerings. If he or she sees nothing else, the visitor will know what ACME is all about.

The next line should read, "To learn more about ACME's widgets, click here."

The next group of words can be: "Other products produced and distributed by ACME are _____ ." Here list the product categories with links to separate pages.

Any disclaimer or modification goes below these words.

A brief description of ACME Corporation should be included on the index page with the link to a longer, more detailed exposition.

If the company insists on having a more generalized index page, then this copy can go on the jump page.

The most successful landing pages are an extension of the company's unique brand identity. They resemble the company's main website in layout and design.

Effective landing pages should address a visitor's needs first. The best landing pages provide leads with information that is directly relevant to his or her specific needs.

After establishing their value, companies can convey the message that any information the marketer asks for is needed solely to better understand and meet the needs of the prospect. This approach encourages prospects to supply qualifying information.

We know one of the Internet's true pioneers, Bob Heyman. He has been involved with it since the first commercial applications appeared in the early 1990s.

He talks often of the need for usability in the website. By usability he is referring to the navigation. It should be simple, straightforward and lead the visitor to the information he or she desires in less than four clicks.

In marketing to small business leaders, the focus should be on "stickiness" – getting visitors to delve deeper to other relevant, confidence-building content. As we have argued, the primary motivator in business-to-business purchase decisions is risk, or, put another way, fear of making the wrong decision.

Therefore, one of the key objectives of B2B searchers after they click-through to the site is to evaluate both the company and its offerings.

Website navigation is another way of saying "click ease." No tour through a site should exceed six clicks with the end result being that the visitor has left a call to action for the company to act.

Since small business leaders ultimately seek a solution to a need, their predominant behavior during the purchase research phase is finding information. Their purpose in clicking deeper into a site is one of vetting.

Going deeper into a website is delving more minutely into the information about the product and services. Getting small business leaders to do this is a key objective in any website effort.

The graphics on the pages should reflect the front or index page. Elements of the "header," the top part of the page should extend to every other page.

Graphics should not overpower the content; rather complement them and provide a natural path for the reader to go deeper into the website. Print sizes should be larger than 8-9 points that are normally suggested. We found that by keeping all type at ten points or higher, navigation for small business leaders became easier and increased the average visit from three to four pages.

Many companies believe that small business visitors use and interact with their websites in the same way as visitors from big corporations do. This is where the *Janus Principle* needs to be applied in website development.

The biggest misconception in this respect is that their customers think like they do. Much like any good relationship, they need to put themselves in the small business person's shoes (i.e. the customer). Most marketing professionals are far too "close" to their offering, corporate vernacular, and all things related to their industry. So things like nomenclature and content grouping often fall in line with their corporate focused thinking not the small business users.

Companies are starting to pay more attention to website design and usability, and budget accordingly for those various improvements. Companies are realizing how central their website is for all small business marketing efforts. When examining their efforts, online and offline in how there is usually at least one touch point on the total marketing efforts, they have found that the website must be analyzed as part of any buying cycle.

Ask 100 website developers for a design and there will be 100 solutions. Each of them will be equally as effective or ineffective in drawing and involving small business visitors. Some experts argue that some widely adopted formats make navigation easier, involve the visitor, and sell products better than others. We do not claim to be experts in this area. However, we would like to provide some guidance in creating a successful website to sell to small business leaders.

We believe that to be successful, a small business website should be tailored specifically to small business visitors. However, as programming tools have become more sophisticated, websites can be tailored to give a unique and specific experience to each visitor, based on the visitor's preferences and interests.

For larger companies selling a multitude of products to diverse audiences, current Web technology allows sites to "recognize" each visitor, search their databases and pull up content that best suits each person, thereby treating different people differently and optimizing the opportunity to meet the marketing goal.

Perhaps one of the best such sites for this approach is *Dell*. On this site, the company practices what some experts call one-to-one marketing.

*Dell*'s homepage (www.dell.com) is divided into four main sections for browsing products and services: Home & Home Office; Small Business; Medium & Large Businesses; and Government, Education & Healthcare. Who the visitor is will determine which section you enter. And, obviously, the content in each section differs.

The drawback in this approach is that *Dell* has added at least one click to the information gathering process.

Each second page is different. In fact, the marketing messages will be completely different as well.

What *Dell* did was to group people into various buckets, depending on their needs, and then developed a special message for each group. They created specific paths, or tracks, tailored to each group.

The site is broken up into sections that will contain a unique message for each visitor group.

Whatever methodology is chosen for that index page, the information must create a desire on the part of visitor to learn more and to contact the company.

Here are some other suggestions on how to increase the touch points with visitors.

There is a group of small business leaders who crave technical information. The more a provider shares, the more information the small business leaders want. At the same time, this process draws these visitors more deeply into the sales process.

If the product/service has technical information or specifications that would be of value to prospects, the company should consider sharing this. This is vital because a prospective customer needs any and all pertinent information related to the potential transaction. But only if the visitor shares his or her own valid email address and perhaps three or four other pieces of data.

Another way of moving the sales process is to refer visitors to the company's blog or "ask the expert."

*IBM* provides complimentary business advice from renowned experts, such as Jim Blasingame, through its website offering *"Advice For Your Small Business."*

*Verizon* concentrates its efforts on using actual examples of success stories told by business leaders.

Both methods are viable but the second one fits more closely to our experiences in successful small business marketing.

Giving something away is another method of increasing a visitor's touch point. What the giveaway is depends on the situation and the need.

We always advise clients to give more away in the form of useful information or trial subscriptions. The key to giveaways is presenting something that is desirable but requires the recipient to do something.

At trade shows, inducements are used to encourage people to watch a demo. Our experience has shown that getting attendees to sign-up prior to the show or for a specific time works best.

On a website or other interactive venue, shorter time periods are necessary but the results in terms of leads can be gratifying.

Other marketing counsels suggest bigger prizes given to one or two lucky attendees. This is a decision the company needs to make and perhaps the best thing to do is to test and compare results.

However, when all is said and done, it is what the company does with the contact that really drives home the sale. In this way, the website mirrors all forms of marketing channels.

We believe the key to success on line, as in all other places is the company's ability to utilize the *Janus Principle* to build success.

There are many other online channels to reach small business leaders and below are a few suggestions.

## Microsites

Microsites are page groups of personalized content that marketers can add to websites; they allow B2B marketers to target specific product features or offers to unique buyer segments.

These sites differentiate their visitors by grouping them based on commonalities. They offer different paths and website sections that are unique to each group. And they provide different experiences for different visitors.

They also offer ways in which any website visitor can communicate with the organization, usually through HTML forms. By providing ways for visitors to teach you how to treat them, you are providing extra value. In other words, if all else is equal, and one site "knows" who I am because it asked me via an HTML form and thereby offers a customizable experience, but another site does not... guess which website I am more likely to visit?

A customizable experience can be achieved by encouraging your website visitor to fill out a form to create a profile of themselves. Whether or not a website is as usable as Dell.com, a one-to-one marketing website anticipates and provides relevant and personal information to each visitor. The anticipation exists because the visitor has filled out a profile or gone to a website section labeled for specific interests, so the website treats him or her differently from other visitors. It's relevant and personal because it speaks to each person's varying needs, desires, functions and preferences.

In short, a site that is anticipated to be relevant and personal to its visitors is going to be more successful in gaining traffic, keeping visitors, creating repeat visitors, creating sales leads and ultimately sales. One-to-one marketing websites offer more value than other websites.

## One Searcher. Multiple Searches.

Small business leaders permit the buying cycle to last months or even years. That's because their purchases undergo much more scrutiny throughout all phases of the buying cycle – and in those phases the same person may perform multiple searches, each with a different intent.

In the first phase (**research**), the purchaser is seeking alternatives, seeing who's out there to potentially fill the need. During this phase the small business leader may use generic search terms related to the product or services sought in order to form a short list of potential providers.

Later, in the **evaluation** stage of the buying cycle, the purchaser's focus turns from researching potential suppliers to researching specific issues related to the product or service, such as performance, efficiency, maintenance, ergonomics, White Papers. Different search terms will be used and different sites will be found and different suppliers may be unearthed, supplanting those previously identified.

Late in the process, just prior to the purchase decision **confirmation**, the searcher has by then a thorough understanding of specific needs, wants, and issues affecting the purchase decision. One last round of searching will likely ensue to confirm the purchaser's intended direction, and again different search terms may be used.

## One Prospect. Multiple Searchers.

Besides internal staff and professional contacts, the typical small business purchase may be influenced by multiple parties throughout the buying cycle, each with the ability to easily research and evaluate purchase alternatives.

The **user buyer** wants to know how the product will improve day-to-day operations. They usually compare it to current operations.

The **technical buyer** is charged with ensuring the product meets established specifications. In this case, comparison with current technology is often done.

The **economic buyer** is concerned with ROI and other financial matters. This often comes down to a case of current costs versus fure savings.

The prospect may also have engaged consultants or "coaches" that help the company with the decision-making process.

Today, each of these parties has the ability to quickly and easily research purchase alternatives and vet purchase recommendations with a few clicks of the mouse; and all use varying search terms depending on their role and their specific concerns. Although one person may have spent weeks doing purchase research, a functional head who spends 15 minutes on Google can raise enough questions to dramatically alter the organization's purchase decisions.

Good small business search engine optimization considers the different influencers and the search terms they are likely to use, and has landing pages that speak to the various influencers.

## Search Engine Optimization (SEO)

For the reasons outlined above, search engine optimization (SEO) is another element in the selling process.

Much has been written about search engine optimization and no doubt much more will be authored. Nobody has the complete answer and there are no shortcuts. SEO is a continuing process. Recognizing the importance of SEO is an important part of the website development process.

The goal of most small business leaders that conduct searchers is research:

→ They seek the best potential suppliers, evaluate their experience, determine the key decision issues in choosing a supplier, and reduce the chances of making the wrong choice.

The company's goal, on the other hand, is to identify who the website visitors are and to develop a relationship with them. This relationship enables the company build credibility and be positioned as a preferred provider while letting the visitor get to know about its products and have confidence in the provider. This process takes time, effort and trial and errors. Moreover, it is not perfect and will continually change as the Internet changes.

It has been suggested that the goal of search engine optimization for marketers is not an immediate sale but, rather, inclusion in the consideration set, the short list of preferred suppliers from which the ultimate provider will be selected.

We agree but hold out hope that some visits contribute to the sales cycle better than others.

Conversion in the small business sector is usually not immediate; nor does conversion typically occur online. In small business search engine optimization, getting found is just the beginning.

Whether the company seeks searchers or buyers, it's important to understand the search terms prospects may be using in the different phases of the buying cycle. With a good understanding of this, the company can use SEO to ensure that the website is not only initially found but also getting referred to at every search conducted in the buying cycle.

There are many good books and online information about SEO in general and choosing search words in particular. One technique we have found particularly helpful is to examine our web analytics to see which words were used to find our website.

The list of search words always contains a surprise or two. And it varies from month to month.

Keyword strategy is critical to successful business-to-business SEO. Make sure that the company takes the time to fully explore and select the potential terms that searchers are likely to use in the purchasing process, and design your site accordingly.

Build into the landing pages carefully chosen links to other content that will build credibility and get the company in the consideration set.

In addition to creating strong content, use a good web analytics program to help evaluate stickiness factors, such as length and depth of visits, time spent on specific pages, and whether the number of return visitors is growing.

The words that you use both in on-page and off-page (meta tags) copy have significant influence on rankings in the search engine results. Experts like Bob Heyman argue that the nature of copy is very important in small business search engine optimization. Not only does Web page copy need to influence ranking in the search engine results, it must also persuade the business purchaser.

We do not intend to go deeper into this sector because there are more detailed offerings and experts with more specific expertise available. One person we think is particularly knowledgeable is Gary Angel, founder and President of SEO Search.

One last thought. Study the website's analytics and begin to understand where visitors are coming from, what they do on the site, where they leave from and where they go. Over time, patterns will emerge that can help the company build an effective website for the small business sector.

## Converting the Small Business Visitor

The objective of good websites is to sell products or services. If the website itself does not offer goods or services, it will somehow find ways of identifying visitors and getting sales motivating information to them.

Companies in the small business space often believe that they can sell a product or service through the website. This process is called "conversion."

Measurement of conversion varies by company, product/service, audience or even season. The important element in conversion is building a rapport or relationship with the small business leader.

Conversion is a relationship-building process that requires numerous touch points and interactions. It takes place over time in a variety of online and offline encounters. The company must focus on increasing the number and quality of those encounters by offering opportunities for the visitor to be engaged.

Ideally, search engine optimization helps to create not only the first encounter but also multiple subsequent encounters throughout the buying cycle.

The use of "cookies" to identify returning visitors and greeting them by name is just one of the ways of building rapport.

But getting visitors to the company website is not enough. There must be a rich vein of materials to engage and encourage the visitor to return again and again. Besides White Papers, these engagement tools include: blogs, surveys, social networks and proprietary information available conveniently at the website.

Measuring success is usually by convincing the visitor to leave his or her email address and perhaps some other information, such as title, company name, responsibilities and other tidbits. From these information clusters, other touch points can be developed such as minisites, surveys, special online seminars, newsletters and other information sharing activities.

Another approach is to offer the visitor access to a part of the website that is not open to the general population. In this section, proprietary information and special announcements can be communicated to the visitor in exchange for more information.

Ultimately, the result of this approach is a sale either via the Internet or more probably through personal contact.

## Electronic Newsletters

Each month, *Information Strategies, Inc.* sends out more than five million electronic newsletters to its small business audience. Many open them immediately, others later in the week and still more never. Over the years, we have built a rapport with these readers by offering actionable information.

This audience grew from a base of 385,000 records supplied by a third party. Most came by way of viral marketing. That is, our readers referred them to us.

Small business leaders need information and suggestions to build their enterprises. By creating an electronic newsletter that provides valuable, usable information, the company can build a similar rapport. The newsletter should not be a puff-piece but rather offer advice and guidance based on the company's expertise. The information included should be timely and appeal to the target audiences needs,

While it is always tempting to "blow our own horns," the best approach is to subtly demonstrate our relevance with valuable, proprietary content. Within most companies, there is a repository of expertise that can be mined for this process.

The electronic newsletter should appear regularly and have the ability to be sent to other online visitors by the recipient.

Results often take time but usually end up growing the list of potential buyers and expanding the reach of the website and by extension, the company.

For details on how to set up and run a newsletter, see our chapter on emailing.

## White Papers

Another adage we hear often is "An expert is anyone 50 miles from home."

While the Internet is on one's desk the information may originate thousands of miles away. Therefore, it is possible to generate positive images of the company simply by demonstrating its expertise in a variety of ways.

The best forum and one in which the company is in total control is the White Paper.

There are three elements in a White Paper that make them more appealing to small business leaders. They are:

→ Is the information relevant to their needs, desires or fears?
→ Who is the author and why is he or she offering this information?
→ Is the content credible?

A White Paper should provide information that is relevant to each reader in the context of his or her position and needs. The offering needs to address one area and be clear about its objectives. Preferably, it should address an issue that is facing the small business leader and it should offer solutions.

A White Paper that addresses an issue or issues that tend to create fear in small business leaders is more apt to get their attention than a White Paper focusing on a need or desire. For instance, one of our clients created a monograph on the five financial activities a small business should do to weather a recession. The heads of two small businesses wrote the suggestions and a Harvard economics professor was its editor.

This monograph satisfied all three requirements mentioned above. The information provided was relevant to the needs and fears of the audience. The authors were small business leaders just like the audience and a Harvard professor vetted it. Finally, the content was viewed as credible because it was written and edited by individuals outside the firm.

If the company wants to use in-house staff for the White Paper, it is helpful to have an outside source or vetting authority. This lends credibility in addition to adding to the overall professionalism to the piece. This approach is effective if a survey is created and then conducted by an independent research group.

Many Internet experts disagree on the following point. Often visitors must provide an email address in order to download the White Paper. This reduces the number of downloads but does generate leads.

No matter what the approach, White Papers do provide a solid channel to generate "touches" and positive feelings from small business leaders.

## Web Conferencing and Podcasts

The Internet has become a highway to many new channels to touch small business leaders. Among the fastest growing channels are web seminars and podcasts. They have become a cost-effective methodology to reach potential clients with the company's message.

We describe web conferencing as live meetings or presentations over the Internet and podcasts as an informational broadcast to be automatically transferred to a mobile device after they are downloaded. The latter has become increasingly popular in education.

Web conferencing spans from a webcast (which is typically one-way, from the speaker to the audience with limited audience interaction) to a "webinar" which can be very collaborative and include polling and question-and-answer sessions to allow full participation between the audience and the presenter. There are web conferencing technologies that have incorporated the use of VoIP audio technology, to allow for a truly web-based communication.

The former is more interactive with participants and panelists talking to each other simultaneously. We think sponsored web conferences work best in the context of events such as a show or gathering.

Publishing companies, marketing firms, associations and think tanks are all offering web conferencing and podcast platforms to get a client's message across to an audience sitting at their desks, and/or, in the latter case, on the go.

Companies should sponsor these seminars when they have the following attributes:

→ The topic is relevant to the small business audience.
→ The topic provides information addressing needs, desires and fears.
→ The topic is perceived as neutral in delivering the content.

Our clients' experience has been that the closer the topic is to the needs, desires and fears of the small business leader, the greater the participation. Equally as important, the follow-up conversations are more apt to result in sales.

Providing information addressing needs and fears rather than substitution is the most effective use of web seminars. Introducing a new product that requires changes or is not a substitution providing additional profits is not the best use of web seminars.

The utilization of new technology such as web conferencing also brings the added benefit of demonstrating familiarity with new methods and means of communication. Often, this fact alone is enough to attract potential customers who view these innovations as important to the future of their companies.

Try not to be too blatant in the sales pitch within the broadcast but instead use it to establish the company's identity within the community. Web seminars are best used to expand the company's footprint and expertise.

If the company does decide to utilize web conferencing, they should keep podcasts valuable and short, and use newsletters and blogs to promote them. Have people register for them and follow-up with emails and direct mail, the same as you would a live seminar.

One critical aspect of web conferencing and podcasts is the follow-up by the sponsor. Get the list of participants and follow-up with an email and direct mail campaign within four weeks of the broadcast. It can pay rich dividends.

We will mention here a new technology and offering that will have an impact as the years go by. There is a company called *The Ribbon* (www.ontheribbon.com) that offers companies the ability to provide real time television over the Internet for seminars and demonstration session.

The company's unique technology permits anyone with a computer and telephone hookup (even dial-up) to view the program without the jerkiness attendant to other systems. What's more, there is no special program or set box needed to view these offerings.

We are confident that as time goes on, wider applications such as this will open new doors to marketers aiming at the small business marketplace.

## Social Networks

The Internet is substituting for personal contact in many ways. Perhaps the most obvious manifestation is the social network phenomenon. Facebook now has more than 70 million participants. As we write this book, business-to-business social networks such as *LinkedIn* are growing at a fast clip. We expect their importance to grow over time.

At a recent conference on Internet marketing, a speaker opined that he thought social networks would take the place of User Groups and other information exchange gatherings.

Companies are starting to build in social networks as part of their websites as are colleges, business schools alumni as well.

A Colorado company, *eSocialNetwork* even provides companies with the opportunity to sell products through social networking.

The drawback to social networking is that the company has no control over what is said. The resulting information exchange may be as harmful as it is helpful.

Social networking as a business-to-business channel may have a future but as we write this book, it is in its adolescent stage. Creating a social network within the company's client base is a two-edged sword that can be as harmful as it is helpful.

## Blogs

Blogs have been called "citizen journalism." The have added a touch of reality and correction to more traditional journalism that is sorely needed. However, like everything, there are limits that must be placed on these offerings because they can do as much harm as good.

For the company, blogs offer opportunity and danger.

Anyone with a computer and access to an aggregator can get his or her message out to many people. Since negativism sells better than good news, a majority of these bloggers often provide the downside of any event, product, service, or person.

*Apple Computer* has been plagued by a blogger who not only breaks news about its products but also reveals inside information that Apple considers private.

The company sued him but only got more bad publicity. Answering a negative blog from an individual only raises the visibility of the blogger.

On the other hand, if a company creates a blog, the information is viewed with a healthy dose of skepticism. Company blogs are often viewed with suspicion as being a "company newspaper."

The best antidote to negative blogs is good PR. Let other publications tell the company's story.

## Why Business Blog?

Companies that sell primarily to small businesses find that a blog more easily bridges the feedback loop between end customers and channels. For any organization, a blog is part of a long-term customer evangelism strategy.

If your existing company website design is not good or is non-existent, most blog service providers offer good-looking templates to use. In comparison to high-functioning websites, Blogs are easy to set-up and pay for. Two providers consider are *www.Blogger.com*, which is a free service, and *www.TypePad.com*, which is offered through a monthly or annual subscription.

## The Value of Advertising on Business Blogs

Blogs provide advertisers an opportunity to reach a devoted audience niche if they are compelling, and written by recognized experts in a narrow niche.

With click-through rates in traditional online advertising dropping, inexpensive blog click-throughs are as high as 1%. Advertisers are starting to appreciate the influencer constituency on blogs, where the advertising value can provide an emotional appeal.

You can create a blog advertising campaign that will have great impact for less than the cost of a single ad in a national print magazine.

| GOOD, EFFECTIVE ADS | POOR, LOW/NO-RESPONSE ADS |
| --- | --- |
| → Interesting images | → Dull, text-heavy content |
| → Multiple links | → No links |
| → Use video or audio | → Tell, rather than show; few/no images |
| → Hand-made feel | → Feels "designed" |
| → Puzzle/question invites click | → Full pitch negates click |
| → Use of metaphors, examples, recommendations | → Pushing a product rather than an experience |

## RSS Feeds

*Information Strategies, Inc.* was one of the earliest users of RSS feeds for our small business websites. RSS (Really Simple Syndication or Rich Site Summary) is an XML-based format for easily distributing and aggregating Web content (such as headlines). RSS feeds are not only a way of getting information quickly and in digest form, they also offer an opportunity to send a company's message out to others in a meaningful and timely format. RSS feeds also can be used as antidote to negative blogs and a positive method of attracting visitors.

By bringing an RSS feed onto the website, companies can add to their websites' content (web pages, PR releases, White Papers, etc.) and provide a way of constantly updating the audience as well as the website.

On a personal level, users determine their favorite websites and properly configured RSS aggregator will syndicate selected lists of hyperlinks and headlines, along with other information about the websites, then display the contents on the user's desktop at regular intervals. The user decides to follow the link or not.

## Wikis

There is an old sales adage that goes "The more the prospect talks, the quicker the sale."

Wikis give prospects the opportunity to talk. Wikis also give the company exposure on the Web, help build communities, obtain collaborative brainstorming, and improve search engine ranking through additional Wiki links.

Companies are starting to use Wikis as a means of drawing in new clients, learning from existing customers and growing their own knowledge base.

There is a drawback to Wikis for the company.

The fundamental premise behind a Wiki is that anyone can edit any page. For that to work, the company needs to have trust, which is usually found in tight communities. As the Wiki grows that community becomes larger and the chances of salacious or negative comments appearing grow.

Ward Cunningham, developer of the first Wiki software, describes the essence of the Wiki concept as follows:

> "A Wiki invites all users to edit any page or to create new pages within the wiki website, using only a plain-vanilla web browser without any extra add-ons.
>
> Wiki promotes meaningful topic associations between different pages by making page link creation almost intuitively easy and showing whether an intended target page exists or not.

A Wiki is not a carefully crafted site for casual visitors. Instead it seeks to involve the visitor in an ongoing process of creation and collaboration that constantly changes the website landscape."

A company can build those communities on the open Internet, but they are definitely rare. Wikipedia has successfully managed to build a community of trust. However, as it has grown bigger, problems have arisen in terms of accuracy, and opinion taken as fact.

Wikis offer a medium for collaborative brainstorming. Proposing a new product on a Wiki and asking comments can lead to interesting, valuable feedback. For instance, suggesting a name and learning that in Thailand it means "horror."

Like many things on the web, given its ability to draw in diverse audiences, wikis can help and also hinder. Be careful of what you wish, you may get it and realize it is not what you really wanted to hear or have broadcasted.

## Viral Marketing

Through viral marketing, we at *ISI* have grown our database, in five years, to more than five million readers.

Viral marketing is based on a simple premise: "If you build something of value and desire, people will come."

At the turn of the 20$^{th}$ century trolley routes out of American towns usually ended at a dirt field. A whole generation of entrepreneurs built amusement parks and other attractions at the end of the line. Often, traction companies financed them in an effort to increase riders, especially on weekends when traffic was light.

The Internet is the new trolley lines, websites the destinations and viral marketing the tool that brings visitors. For the company seeking small business leaders as visitors, viral marketing is a cost effective strategy.

There are three keys to successful viral marketing:

➤ Attention getting material in the content sent out.

→ Useful content on the website that encourages deeper diving by visitors.
→ Continual updating that encourages (demands) repeated visits.

Viral marketing is about creating great web content that small business leaders want to consume (and share with others) rather than coercing them to fill out a form to get something. Viral marketing success comes from self-publishing Web content that small business leaders want to share. It is not about gimmicks. It is not about paying an agency to coerce people into doing something. It is not about using something like a White Paper as "lead bait."

Any given story, concept, report, analysis, survey will attract respondents to a greater or lesser degree. Viral marketing is about creating content that others want to read and share. It is also about getting these readers to visit a website and return again and again.

For some viral marketing leaders, this visitor group centers on a buyer persona. This is essentially a demographic group of buyers that the company has identified as having a specific interest in the organization or product or a specific market problem that the product solves.

By doing some basic research on current buyers (just listen to them!) and then creating content that appeals to them, the company's viral marketing efforts will be much more effective.

Viral marketing is effective with targeted content (an e-book, an interactive tool, a social media application, a blog, or a contest) developed for specific buyer personas. At the same time, this more focused content will also improve search engine optimization because the words and phrases used in the copy are targeted specifically to a specific sector or need. Naturally, any identified problems can be solved with the company's products/services.

As we indicated earlier when talking about a website, it is not enough to get a visitor to the door it is getting them to come in and return again. Many first time visitors will be non-clients that won't spark any interest; a few will generate some notice and basically pay back your investment of the time required to create them; and a handful will go viral and make the entire program of ten or twenty viral marketing campaigns worthwhile.

Viral marketing is not about sales leads. It is about spreading ideas. Step back for a moment and consider the company's goals in planning a viral marketing initiative.

With viral marketing, forget about leads and focus on spreading the news about the company and its ideas. Whenever possible, make information totally free with no registration required. Give away that e-book or White Paper. Point people to free video and audio.

Since companies insist on measuring ROI, there are some things that can be used as metrics. They include:

- Number of people exposed to your ideas.
- The frequency bloggers are talking about the company and its offerings.
- What these bloggers are saying about the company.
- The website's ranking in search results for important phrases.
- The number of small business leaders that are engaging and choosing to speak about the company's offerings.
- Viral marketing spreads the company's ideas so that people find it.

## Radio Broadcasting

Early in the 1990s a very smart Philadelphia marketing consultant showed us the most cost effective media to reach small business owners – radio.

Further, he showed us how to purchase time on these programs cheaply.

This guru, who is now gone, explained that many small business leaders listened to the rebroadcasts of popular daytime commentators at night. He also pointed out that clear channel stations, the powerful 50,000-watt broadcasters, covered 90% of the country at night with their signals.

For his marketing to small business clients, he purchased these rebroadcast times and midnight airings of other programs at rates often 70% below what they would have cost during the day.

His ROI doubled or tripled using this technique.

Even if the company chooses to purchase radio during the day, it is one of the most cost-effective methods to reach small business leaders. It is a fact that the audiences of certain commentators are heavy with the individuals small business marketers want – small business leaders. They are expensive to use but can deliver sales.

In our discussions with companies looking to reach these leaders, we have seen a marked reluctance to utilize these conservative commentators. There is some bias involved along with a feeling that somehow the audience is more radical than it actually is.

However, listening to one or two broadcasts should dispel this notion as their roster of advertisers is a who's who of brands. Their media buying agencies know that these programs deliver.

Again, remember that the message must be consistent across all media but radio is our recommended second best source of sales.

## Use Radio Talk Shows to Your Advantage

Radio talk shows that feature conservative commentators are a strong channel to small business leaders, who make up a significant portion of their audience.

Here are some of the top syndicated radio talk shows that are popular among small business leaders:

→ *The Mike Gallagher Show:* Talk show host Mike Gallagher has one of the fastest growing talk shows in America.

→ *The Radio Factor with Bill O'Reilly:* For two hours each weekday, more than 400 stations broadcast one of the most successful radio shows in the nation.

→ *The Rush Limbaugh Show:* most listened to radio talk show in America, broadcast on over 600 radio stations nationwide.

→ *Jim Cramer's Real Money:* Cramer is a well respected financial talk show host.

→ *Michael Savage:* Political and social commentary with bite but a very responsive audience.

→ *The Laurie Roth Show:* Broadcasts to over 45 stations nationally on the USA Radio Network and the National Radio Network.

→ *Moneytalk with Bob Brinker:* One of the most respected financial talk show hosts. **His radio show is syndicated by ABC Radio.**

Spend some time listening to those radio talk shows, and consider buying ad time on the ones you feel will help you reach your target audience.

One publication you might want to subscribe to is *TALKERS magazine,* the leading trade publication serving the talk radio industry in America. It has been dubbed "The Bible of Talk Radio" by *Business Week* magazine. As technology and media trends have evolved, the publication has expanded to serve the cutting edge of the "New Talk Media" which includes talk on the Internet as well as cable television.

*TALKERS magazine* publishes ten issues annually, and subscriptions cost $75 per year. The magazine features news stories about the non-stop happenings in talk radio and the new talk media including articles about top hosts and stations, developments at the networks, interviews with movers and shakers, the opinions of industry participants and leaders, and fast-breaking developments in technology.

Aside from radio industry news, the publication also conducts ongoing research of the topics and opinions discussed and expressed on hundreds of talk stations and programs across the United States and compile them into surveys and graphs, which have become the standard of the industry.

That is but one of the many trade publications that you should be reading on a regular basis.

## Internet Radio

All of these radio hosts have websites. These websites are rapidly becoming an effective auxiliary channel to small business leaders. If you recall, we said that many of them listen as they work at night. Often, they turn to these websites to hear the rebroadcast of that day's live program.

Purchasing time on the rebroadcast or on the web pages is a very cost effective avenue to reach them. We have a client who uses this approach to reach small business owners for life and surviving partnership insurance.

In the coming years, we expect this avenue to grow as a small business channel. Because many small business leaders listen late at night, it is important to have telephone coverage when these ads run.

## Television and Cable

Given the expense of television and cable, it is a medium often left to national brands. Television is a mass medium designed to inform rather than motivate to buy. Nonetheless, some products have flourished using television as an avenue to sales.

In most cases these products have satisfied a desire rather than a need. Two examples, first, the Rosetta Stone company sells language learning made simple. Second, another company offers disks to teach individuals the use of specific computer programs.

For several clients, we have investigated television as a launched media and recommended against it. There is one statistic that glares out at us from our surveys of small business leaders: they watch about four hours of television a week. This is less than half the national average.

We have used local cable effectively to backstop a marketing effort centered on a particular locale. Ads on some cable outlets are as low as $15 per unit. At this price, and in late night business shows (or repeats of daytime offerings), they may be a possible venue.

Overall, television and cable do not represent the most cost effective channels to reach small business leaders.

## Telephone

The first known telephone book was published in 1878, just two years after Alexander Graham Bell called his assistant, Thomas Watson, for the first time.

The 20-page, pamphlet-size book, published by the *Connecticut District Telephone Co.*, contained the names and numbers of 391 New Haven-area subscribers. It also provided some helpful hints to callers: "Should you wish to speak to another subscriber you should commence the conversation by saying 'Hulloa!'"

There were other tidbits of advice included in the book, including one that limited calls to three minutes unless it was an emergency.

Since Watson's summons by Bell, billions, if not trillions, of people have been called to, scolded, cajoled, wooed, loved, hated, heartbroken, and generally informed by the telephone.

Small business leaders view the telephone for the most part as a blessing and a curse. A blessing as it is a lifeline for new sales and also a Trojan horse of bothersome interruptions.

In our surveys of leaders of both large and small organizations, we have seen one significant fact. Whereas the small business often answers the phone with a live person, a larger organization uses voice mail.

This was brought strikingly home to us when a major supplier and ally was acquired by a bigger firm. For years, the smaller entity had a receptionist who was friendly and helpful, and always had a wealth of information at her figertips. She always made the company's customers feel comfortable and that they were valued, and if someone was not there when they called, she assured them that a message would reach them promptly.

As part of this screening process, she handled the daily cold calls that came in from people selling telephone services, healthcare insurance, leasing programs and the like.

Because she also knew what the company needed, while screening the calls, she also acted as a gatekeeper, letting in cold callers who had a service that was needed.

After the acquisition, that receptionist survived for about three months before she was let go. Suffice it to say the company now has a voice mail system that allows a cold caller to dial in and pick-up names to call.

It is ironic that a methodology used to reduce unwanted calls can also impede the process.

Recently, we were taken on a tour of a large facility that does nothing but identify names, titles and extension numbers of corporate employees.

This facility is run by a grizzled veteran of the search world who made his first million dollars purchasing printed corporate telephone books. In recent years, due to rising costs and technological innovation, these books have gone out of fashion and the electronic telephone listing has come to the fore.

Our friend, Harry, has ways of gaining access to that directory and find the names, title and extension of just about any one in the Fortune 2000 list. He claims more than 100,000 firms in his database.

When it comes to smaller companies, Harry admits some frustration because they generally pick up their phones.

For these entities, his staff works at night, after midnight actually, because it is quite possible that there will be people at the office late at night.

"If my people call to get into the directory and a person answers, we know it's a smaller firm and more importantly, we need to have a ready answer for when asked why we are calling so late," Harry says.

The good news in telephone marketing is that small business leaders pick up their phone. The bad news is that the caller has just ten seconds to gain his or her interest.

In a roundabout way, we have come back to some truths of about selling to small business leaders. They include:

- → Get personal, use proper names and be specific.
- → Have something to say, say it well.
- → Say it in more than one medium.
- → Build rapport, and learn to use effective telephone techniques to gain information.
- → Using the telephone.

The worst form of marketing to small business is starting off the conversation by asking "to speak with the person in charge of telephone service."

These and similar requests for accounting, IT, office supplies and their ilk represent the common form of telephone solicitations. Given the number of such calls our company gets, and reported by other firms, this approach must be working.

Again talking to our friend Harry and others in the industry, we have been told that this sales approach is a numbers game. One sales manager said his hit ratio was 73-1, meaning his staff called 73 companies to get one person to talk to. Of those spoken to, one in five agreed to either an appointment or more material. The close ratio from this point was one in two.

If you do the math, this means a successful telephone operation will need to make 365 calls to earn at least one sale. With the automated dial systems available today, the price of these calls can be as low as $.15/touch.

Two imperatives drive this approach, according to these experts.

The caller must be American; and two, the message needs to be compelling and stated in the first 15 words.

These professional phone marketers tell us that for selling efforts aimed at small business leaders, they find the hit rate goes up when they utilize American voices.

Interestingly, as they moved operations into rural areas to keep costs down, they have found that their hit rates have gone up. They deduce that this is because the voices are more neutral and "American-sounding."

Our friend Harry laughs and says his best operators are convicts working at prisons but because of security and other reasons, he carefully partitions his work consoles so that they do not see the names or addresses of the respondents.

Another imperative is that the message must be delivered in the first few words.

Obviously, "reducing your telephone costs," "improving your shipping efforts," "cutting local inventory taxes," and "protecting your data" are compelling arguments for the conversation to continue.

There are several types of telephone canvassing – getting appointments, selling product, driving customers to stores.

The most difficult is getting appointments and these calls need to have more information available to the caller. For small business leaders to give an appointment, they need to be convinced in the first 30 seconds.

A telephone maven we know breaks these 30 seconds into two parts – the hook and the set. The first ten seconds are the hook when attention is gained.

The next 20 seconds are devoted to setting that hook.

Recently, we had an individual call our company and state simply "We protect your firm from thieving employees." This was the hook. The set came with his next line, "are you confident your employees are cheating you? We have a five minute program that answers that question." He claims a 50% success rate for this approach when he reaches the top manager, particularly among small business leaders.

Selling product over the phone is getting more difficult by the year. One reason is the many scam artists who call and tell a company their order is on the dock and wants payment.

In New Jersey, two men sold more than $2 million in unwanted merchandise in this way. They did it because they spoke with confidence, assurance and a degree of persistence that often convinced even hardened small business owners that they had, indeed, ordered the material.

Tone is important in telephone calling and while it represents only 38% of the total communication process, experts say, on the phone it is more like 50%.

Demonstrating product knowledge as well as knowing something about the client is equally important.

We have a friend who sells inserts into coupon envelopes sent to residents in the Bergen County, New Jersey area. Living in the area he serves allows him to subscribe to all the local newspapers and he goes through them to identify potential clients.

His most effective icebreaker is to call a company that has just won an award or donated to a local activity. This approach usually gives him the name of the highest purchasing person in the small business – the president/owner.

He gets through to this target person by saying he wants to talk about the reward, activity. Once to the individual, he starts his conversation by congratulating him (or her) on the award and suggesting how it might be leveraged into additional sales. His success ratio is usually above 75%.

If you recall, we said that a lot of small business leader marketing centers on being local.

*Lowe's* has developed an excellent program that combines three factors we consider important in marketing to small business leaders – multi-channel approaches, locality and follow-up.

This hardware, gardening and tool supplier utilizes a three-fold approach to add traffic in the store and build up its store card business.

Within a given locality homes and businesses are sent letters offering a store card long with incentives to purchase.

Within two weeks, a telephone call is made to the targeted customer who is requested by name. Word-of-mouth is also generated because many targeted customers receive the offering together and there is always some discussion.

We are told that among targeted individuals who talk to others about the offer, there is an 81% conversion rate. The local *Lowe's* outlets also see increased traffic.

One last thought concerns the lists purchased to drive the marketing calls. They should have been updated within the last three months, include name, address, title, and an accurate phone number. Choosing the right list and testing the script and approach will improve any effort.

The common factors in all of these efforts are what we said earlier:

→ Successful telephone marketers get personal, use proper names and are specific when talking to potential clients.

→ They have something to say that satisfies the need and greed of the targeted individual.

→ They use multiple media to reinforce the message and build "buzz."

→ They find ways of building rapport in the first 30 seconds and establish reasons to buy.

→ Like other media, telephone marketing to small business is a numbers game that requires persistence, personality and a sell message that is honed over hundreds of calls.

## Out-of-Office

On lazy, hazy summer afternoons at many ocean beaches, bathers and sun worshipers can look up and see planes dragging huge signs about local attractions, cars, telephones and a myriad of other offerings.

Researchers have determined that viewership from the ground is almost 100% and recall in the high 80s. Despite the proliferation of cell phones, what this media lacks is an expectation of immediate action by the audience.

Nonetheless, this venue is a "touch" and helps build recognition and eventually activity.

Marketing efforts aimed at small business leaders need to consider these out-of-office venues when building their "seven-touch strategies." To do this, a marketer needs to think creatively. For example, we talked earlier about putting a message on pizza boxes. This is one of the many useful media available.

The next sections will talk about out-of-office venues open to marketers that encourage a call-to-action on the part of targeted clients.

One place to start is the local movie theater. Once a haven from commercials, they are now a venue for them that is gradually winning acceptance from audiences.

Admittedly, most theater audiences are made up of younger people but by carefully choosing the movies that appeal to older audiences, they have a value. This approach is particularly useful if localized campaigns are being used.

## Trains, Planes and Buses

The song about trains, plains and buses signals other venues that offer touch points to small business leaders.

Trains, both commuter and long distance, are used by small business leaders and their staffs to a greater extent than the general population. Signs inside commuter cars are a way of raising visibility.

On long-distance trains, Amtrak has a pocket magazine that is a cost effective vehicle. Professional ridership is up on trains, and this media offers a good venue.

At stations, usually where these two transportation offerings meet, the ad signs are read. In all transportation advertising there should be a reward for taking action, either a free gift, analysis, White Paper, or other giveaway. There should be an easy-to-remember number such as *1-800-Flowers.*

Planes and their terminals are another choke point for advertising. Although expensive, advertising in airline magazines is effective.

Studies by these publications show a very high rate of readership by passengers. Interestingly, business travelers often bring work on the plane and not alternative reading material. When delays happen, and they are happening more frequently, they often turn to the seat pocket for reading material.

Again, advertising to this audience should include a reward for acting.

Buses roll right by the window of small business leaders. Signage on these moving billboards gets the message out to this target audience. The signage should also contain an easy-to-remember media for reaching the advertiser.

## Billboards, Restaurants, Hotels and Motels

Billboards are expensive and they waste audience, but they do attract attention. Financial institutions have long proved that they reach small business leaders. For introducing a product/service to a wide audience quickly, they are unsurpassed. Drivers want distractions, particularly in heavy traffic so they offer a can't-miss way of "getting the message out to a broad audience."

Restaurants and diners are still favored meeting places for small business leaders. They often use them in place of office visits or conferences. As a result, they can serve as another advertising venue. In Tarrytown, NY, there is a diner called El Dorado that is at the confluence of several major highways.

Everyday, small business managers use it as a locale for meetings. The placemats provided by the diner have advertisements. Just outside the inner door is a rack of business cards offering everything from IT services to water damage clean-up.

For years, *American Express* utilized the payment counter as a place to offer sign-up brochures for their products. Lately, due to high print and paper costs, we have seen this valuable space deserted but we are told that the company will be back in force.

Hotels and motels are another advertising venue that should be considered. Most small business leaders stay at the lower cost chains that are always open to new revenue sources.

One other venue to consider is the packets given out by rental companies. They too have been cutting back on these packets because of costs but here is another way of touching the small business leader.

## Cell Phones, Blackberries and Texting

As we write this book, advertising through cell phones and Blackberries is growing as a sales venue. This is the ultimate out-of-office medium with a channel to immediately respond. In today's marketplace, businesses must be creative in order to reach small business leaders. One of the newest ways to reach busy small business leaders wherever they are in their busy lives is through mobile technology. Companies are turning to texting via cell phones and PDAs to enhance marketing efforts.

Texting can be used as a way to reach small business owners/managers in a personalized manner without the time and cost involved in a face-to-face meeting. However, in order for it to be successful, companies need to do some preparation and planning ahead of time. The road to successful texting should include:

**Defining the Goal and Considering the Options:** First, the company needs to clearly identify its goal/purpose for reaching out to small business leaders. Is it to share information about products or services available? Is it to provide technical support?

Is it to focus on one particular marketing campaign? Options could include the ability for customers to buy products via their cell phone or PDA or for the company to share new products/specials with consumers via a text announcement or even for consumers to have the ability to receive real-time customer support from a company's technical department.

This goal should change over time as the company gets more successful with this type of marketing. For example, a company may start out by using texting in a very basic way, such as by generating an order confirmation or shipping notice to consumers. Then once that is being successfully and widely used, the company might move to offering the ability to receive specials via texting and then finally, offer the ability to order products and services.

**Knowing the Target Audience**: Along with identifying the goal/purpose, it's also important for the company to know their audience. This could include the average age of the business owner/ manager, the size of the company, the industries they are in, the locations involved. The better a company knows the potential audience, the better chance the marketing initiative will succeed.

**Planning an Initiative:** Once the goal has been established and the audience is known, it's time to plan how the news of the new marketing strategy will be shared with those target small business leaders. The success of the campaign will depend on getting the word out about the option for texting. It also depends on showing consumers how it will benefit them specifically and not just the company.

**Building the Subscriber List:** The final preparation step involves creating the list of people that will be involved in the project. Companies can share the option and benefits with current customers through newsletters, mailings, phone calls and offer the ability for the consumer to sign up for the list.

It will generally be more successful if a company creates a list from existing customers and internal outreach strategies. However, another option is to share small business leaders lists with a company that has a similar target audience and try to leverage those small business leaders into choosing to also join the company's texting base. Per the Mobile Marketing Association (MMA), it is currently a violation of the code of conduct to purchase a list of subscribers for use in this type of marketing strategy.

**Sending Out Brief Messages that Create Value:** Companies should focus on sending out texting messages that are brief and to-the-point since they will be viewed on a small phone or PDA screen. The messages should never be more than 2-3 lines long and should not include abbreviations to save space unless they are very common ones that will be easily understood by the whole audience.

**Marketing at the Right Time:** In addition to length and tone of the message, it is also important to consider the timing as well. While messages can be sent at any time of the day or night, it's important to think about the time when the majority of the owners and managers will be conducting business. For example, a company shouldn't send a text out offering a new product or special price at a time when the company's customer service office is closed and the small business leaders can't receive more information or make a purchase.

**Testing the Process:** The final step before taking this new marketing strategy live is to test the process several times with a small base of small business leaders. Gain the permission of a few trusted customers who are willing to be "guinea pigs" and do several tests. This will not only allow the company to make sure they have the process down, but will also allow them to gain feedback from the users about what's working/not working and what they'd like to see most from future texts.

If a company isn't already using texting as a marketing strategy, they should begin as quickly as possible. There are hundreds of millions of mobile technology users in the United States and companies that aren't reaching out to this group are missing a large small business leaders pool. By following these seven steps, companies will be in a great place to become successful with this type of marketing.

We have given just a taste of the various ways to touch small business leaders. Office supply and other retail outlets are also available to the marketer but with more difficult obstacles for gaining exposure.

These retailers along with the so-called "Big Box" chains such as *Costco* and *Wal-Mart* are rapidly becoming the distribution nodes to small business leaders.

They represent a big channel to this marketplace.


## Retail Outlets and Big Boxes

Stores such as *Staples, Office Max, Costco* and *Wal-Mart* are where smaller business leaders shop. They are a "choke point" that can be used to spread the word about the company's products/services.

At a New Jersey restaurant supply depot, where restaurateurs go for supplies, food and equipment, there is a point-of-purchase display unit at the exit door. Each day, hundreds of potential purchasers pass this display that has a sign indicating the complete system is available for $3,999 for customers of the depot.

It is effective since according to depot management they sell at least one system a week at every location.

*Staples, Office Max, Office Depot* offer the best choke points to reach small business leaders. They also offer a challenge to any new and/or small company in terms of gaining shelf space.

We are not here to go into detail about the sometimes long-term process of gaining shelf space but rather to encourage their use as a marketing channel. While difficult, the rewards are significant.

Don't neglect *Costco* and *Wal-Mart* as outlets as well. Many leaders of smaller enterprises shop these locations and can be influenced to purchase if they see a product/service available through these retailing giants.

Getting that first Big Box is difficult but once the company succeeds, the others will open their shelves.

# SUMMARY

There are many books that talk about changing the organization. Many more talk about how to market products/services.

We have asked the company to do both.

In sections above, we have asked the company to make major changes within itself and in the methodology by which it markets to small business leaders.

Adopting the *Janus Principle* is very demanding of all company employees.

We evolved the *Janus Principle* as a result of our own efforts to reach and market to small business leaders. While the process evolved over time, once understood we have been able to apply it to other organizations.

Based on our experience, most companies fail in the execution of the marketing, rather than the repositioning of the company's efforts.

By devoting a significant portion of the book to the "The How" of marketing to small business leaders we focused on the execution.

We are reminded of the saying that "a critic is like a eunuch. He can tell you a hundred ways of making love but can't do it himself."

In the pages above devoted to executing, we have provided a roadmap for executing the *Janus Principle*. Nothing we suggest is cast in concrete. In addition to difference in industries as well as size of companies, the delivery channels are changing. Because of the Internet and other factors, marketing to small business leaders is an evolving process and one we think will grow even more demanding over time.

Nonetheless, if a company learns to think like its small business leader audience, it will continue to succeed.

The overriding mantra must be to understand the small business leader's primary motivations and address them in a way that leads to a conclusion that the company's product/service is the solution.

The God Janus was the welcoming symbol to a Roman household.

The *Janus Principle* is a methodology to invite small business leaders to the company's precincts. Once inside, the sell process becomes easier and surer.

Like the two-headed god Janus, the company must always have its focus inward and outward to maximize sales and profits.

ADDENDUM

# TEN EFFECTIVE STRATEGIES TO GROW YOUR BUSINESS IN DOWN TIMES

These strategies are suggested by survey respondents and focus group participants contacted by *Information Strategies, Inc. (ISI)* during the last quarter of 2008.

The survey generated more than 320 responses from senior level business leaders.

It was supplemented by focus groups in four major cities and in-depth telephone interviews by staff members.

- ➜ *Strategy 1:* Positive management outlook is a necessary key to survival and growth.
- ➜ *Strategy 2:* Keep your staff and yourself positive and busy.
- ➜ *Strategy 3:* Put yourself in your customers' shoes and act accordingly.
- ➜ *Strategy 4:* Know where you stand in the changing purchasing hierarchy.
- ➜ *Strategy 5:* The best defense is a good offense but don't be too far ahead of the crowd.

→ *Strategy 6:* Talk more with your current client base and learn what their needs are.

→ *Strategy 7:* Closely manage accounts receivable, inventory and accounts payable.

→ *Strategy 8:* Strive to put more value into product/service offerings before cutting prices.

→ *Strategy 9:* Stick with what the company knows best and don't be too quick to jump.

→ *Strategy 10:* Be proactive and position the company for growth now and in the future.

## Introduction

Most business leaders can make money during boom times. It is the creative, smart business leaders who grow during economic downturns.

Identifying the ways and means of being successful in this time of contracting economics is the driving force behind these suggested strategies.

Boom times generate opportunities and resources. Economic downturns create an atmosphere of fear that stifles both opportunities and dries up resources. In good times and bad, growing a business in and of itself is not enough. That growth must generate profits as well.

Driving profitable growth in both economic climates requires skills that blend aggressive efforts with a strong control of resources. These skills are developed through a combination of learning and doing. One of the best ways is to learn from others who have successfully navigated these perilous times and by trial-and-error in one's own company.

"The Ten Effective Strategies To Grow Your Business In Down Times" benefits from the collective experiences of business leaders across many industrial sectors and differing company sizes. It is based on interviews, surveys and focus groups of business leaders who grew their firms during past down cycles. What sets them apart is the feeling that once challenged, they were better able to focus their companies and succeed where others had faltered.

From these inputs are distilled the rules which are offered as a roadmap for other managers seeking to navigate what promises to be one of the most difficult periods in recent memory. Like any roadmap, the reader is encouraged to view these rules as guides, to be followed but also adopted, and even ignored, in response to individual circumstances.

A downturn can be the best of times for those who see opportunity instead of roadblocks. That's why the opening lines to *A Tale of Two Cities* offers a good starting point for this book. "It was the best of times. It was the worst of times." As Dickens points out in his fable of the French Revolution, bad times bring out the best and worst in us.

This trait applies to individuals as well as companies. It is why the survivors of the Great Depression of the 1930's often remember the working together as well as the heartache. What most successful people who came out of the Depression focused on was finding opportunity in a time of despair.

However, not every one had happy memories and not all saw opportunity in a landscape of failure and fear. This dichotomy is also present today as our own experiences at *Information Strategies, Inc.* reflect. Some of the editors at *ISI* had not experienced bad times. Others have gone through six or seven such periods. Their differing reactions to recent events and those of our readers demonstrates quite clearly that even in the worst of times, successes are possible.

The rules encompassed in this book came about as a result of our staff trying to determine how best to grow our business in the face of adverse conditions. Equally as important, they reflect what our readers told us they had done or were doing to remain viable and growing.

Like our readers, our staff approached the challenges in differing ways. Early on, as the financial crisis broadened, our staff was hearing from many managers about their fears and also their feeling that new opportunities were presenting themselves.

Most of the managers who shared their thoughts reported that they were veterans of at least two such trying periods. In many cases, respondents and participants said they were chastened by each experience, but most also said they expected to face similar challenges in the future.

"The Ten Effective Strategies To Grow Your Business In Down

Times" essentially focuses on six areas:

→ *Managing in a time of stress.*
→ *Identifying internal resources and needs.*
→ *Organizing to expand.*
→ *Focusing on growth without over expanding.*
→ *Evaluating opportunities.*
→ *Managing expectations.*

By using these strategies as a guidepost, you, the reader, can make these worst of times, the best of times.

As with Sydney Carlton, this period can be the best of times and the worst of times.

Which it is for your company, is up to you.

# Strategy 1

*Positive management outlook is a necessary key to survival and growth.*

When Commodore Matthew Perry uttered his famous remark, "Don't give up the ship," a marine in the rigging is reported to have said, "Some people never get the word." Well, Perry won the battle of Lake Erie and with it the entire American Midwest.

The same can be said for other great leaders in times of stress, confusion and despair. Pericles, when asked by the Athenian senate what is the secret of happiness, replied: "The secret of happiness is freedom and the secret of freedom is courage."

In today's world, business leaders must have a sense of courage to continue expanding in the face of daunting obstacles. But this is courage tempered by a clear understanding of the risks involved. In the recent past, the credit market has frozen; consumer spending has tanked, and manufacturing is slowing to a crawl. Into this landscape, a business manager must make critical decisions that affect not only themselves but their employees and the business itself as well.

In bad times, it is easy to "circle the wagons" and "pull in the horns." That course of action is not what a majority of the respondents told *ISI* they did during the last bust cycle.

Many readers may recall that thousands of dot com companies were formed, grew and then died in the last great bust. Many who failed continued to spend beyond all hope of success. The ones that survived husband their resources, rethought their strategies and were positioned to grow as times changed.

The difference between conserving resources and going into a protective shell is often hard to define. One respondent put it simply, "I told my people we wouldn't stop trying harder but we would do it a lot smarter."

There are examples from the more recent past. In the case of this Midwestern manufacturer of kitchen cabinets, the deflation in the building industry hit his company very hard. Orders dropped 55% in the last six months of 2007. His staff of 28 employees began to wonder when some, if not all would be laid off.

This business leader's response to the sales decline was to walk onto the production floor and say he would not be laying off anyone but they would all need to pull together. He was optimistic that his sales staff could bring in new orders, but until then, overtime was out and everyone would need to pitch in and help find ways of cutting costs and reducing waste.

The first quarter of 2008 saw another 10% decline in sales but profits were not down, thanks to the combined efforts of all staffers to find ways of reducing costs. Because management was positive, staff remained upbeat and the company could remain in business until new product offerings kicked in or the industry rebounded.

In the heat of the credit meltdown, a fashion store couple has opened a high-end shop in Boca Raton, Florida. Some may find this foolhardy; others call it daring.

Adversity is the mother of invention. As Christopher Marlowe said in his play, *The Lady Is Not For Burning,* "it is amazing how creative a man becomes when he faces the hangman at dawn. Most businesses do not face such critical decisions, but many are thinking they are as this recession deepens.

# Strategy 2

*Keep your staff and yourself positive and busy.*

In our discussions with business leaders who have survived and grown in previous down cycles there is a recurring message and strategy: "I kept my staff engaged, positive and looking to the future."

Every news report carries details of another company cutting staff. Those who are left behind often betray gallows humor and express fear for themselves.

Even when cuts are made, it is up to management to maintain morale and keep a positive outlook. The Roman army maintained morale by having its legionnaire soldiers build roads and other public works. Companies should adopt this process and utilize downtime to improving physical plant, culling and upgrading prospect lists, reworking equipment and improving product offerings.

Share management concerns, needs and aspirations and have employees suggest solutions. But do so with a sense of purpose and optimism.

In California, a firm that layed off 20% of its workforce maintained morale by having the staff identify new opportunities and offering cash prizes for those who came up with viable solutions.

Get to tasks that are often given short shift in the rush of ordinary business.

One firm in New Jersey is busy reviewing its mailing lists and discovering that there are numerous duplication of addresses and target participants who are no longer at their companies.

Use the time to determine some of the problems affecting customers' usage of your offerings.

Another organization in Ohio has its staff reviewing all customer complaints for the last two years to determine product deficiencies. They have already found five parts that can be reworked and changed at a savings of $30,000 in production costs, not to mention customer satisfaction.

Above all, create a sense of working together to grow when others are being pessimistic.

## Strategy 3

*Put yourself in your customers' shoes and act accordingly.*

Whether you are a BtoB or consumer-centric firm, what you are thinking about in terms of keeping going in a down economy is also happening to your customers.

In a survey taken in late 2008, *ISI* found that more people were optimistic and positive than those negative on their prospects. More than half (57%) of 4,035 business managers said they thought this present situation would last more than a year but 52% said they expected their sales to be up in the coming year. Only 13% said they thought their sales would be down during this period.

This doesn't mean the nation's leaders, pundits and observers are wrong. But many business leaders are very aware of their resources and what it will take to survive. Understanding what they are doing and how it affects your sales efforts is critical.

The best place to start to understand how they are reacting is to look inside your own company. What are you doing to survive? Make a list and then see where your product offerings fit. Also, make a list of your own efforts to weather this downturn.

Compare that list with what you are doing in terms of retrenchment. Armed with this list, do some telephoning and sales calls to find out what your clients are doing. Respondents and focus groups tell us that the two sides, seller and buyer, are very congruent.

With this information in hand, you can then more effectively plan your growth strategy.

## Strategy 4

*Know where you stand in the changing purchasing hierarchy.*

This strategy starts by accepting that purchasing priorities change as economic conditions worsen. Companies must accept that their position within this hierarchy may change and need to have a firm knowledge of where you stand in the purchasing hierarchy.

Many companies start with financial resources. No doubt, you have examined your financial resources. Many companies are focusing on cash flow, a critical element of any business. Many firms report that they are tightening credit and improving collections. Others are postponing capital improvements and new hires. Still others are trimming staff, reducing overtime and looking at small ways of keeping costs down.

Dr. Kenneth E. Lehrer, a Houston economist, looks at purchasing motives in terms of the "A-B-C principle." A's are the things you absolutely must spend on: rent, food, clothes etc. B's are the things you would like to have or do: dine out, magazine subscriptions, cigars. C's are the luxury items you yearn for: boats, recreational vehicles, fine watches.

For companies, there are also A's, B's and C's. A's are the critical items to stay in business: production, rent, staff. B's are the things you should have: insurance, promotion, convention attendance. C's are the things you would like to do: more advertising, added staff, new IT.

In your own business, you have no doubt mentally put the "company spend" on various functions into these terms. Now, put your product offerings in the context of these purchasing criteria and decide where you best fit.

One caveat: you need to be honest in appraising your offerings as to where they best fit. Many of us think our product offerings are a "must have;" but a very wise consultant, David Glickstein, once told us, "Your product is a 'must have' only if not having it will shut down your client's business." Make sure that is the case; if it isn't, decide where your product offerings do fall. Most of us will land in the "nice to have" category. For either of these categories, opportunities abound in a down economy.

For those with "wish-list" type offerings, the challenges are many but still offer opportunities to grow.

# Strategy 5

*The best defense is a good offense but don't be too far ahead of the crowd.*

In our surveys and focus groups, we hear a lot about companies pulling back and retrenching as the economy grows dimmer. At the same time, veterans of other downturns say cutting back is often necessary but it is more important to go on the offensive and "work harder and smarter."

Other respondents tell *ISI* that it is not enough to cut back and reduce expenses, but to be more proactive in the marketplace. This is particularly true in terms of marketing and sales. These firms have returned to fundamentals, and as one Texas executive said, "I am relearning basic tactics that I forgot during good times."

In our focus groups, we have heard five major offensive strategies:

- **Upselling to existing clients.**
- **Repositioning current product/service offerings.**
- **Focusing on sales.**
- **Creating new products.**
- **Restructuring marketing efforts.**

*Upselling to existing clients:* The rule that 80% of sales come from 20% of customers is particularly true in down times.

A retired chief executive of a major marketing firm said he analyzed sales in an earlier recession cycle and found that this to be particularly true. "Ever since then, when times get tough, I go back to my client list; talk to them about their needs and develop strategies to answer them," he said.

One company he advised shifted its marketing effort from new sales prospecting to focusing on already existing clients. "I got their sales staff to switch to talking more with current customers and changed the compensation package to sweeten incentives for additional sales to current clients," he said.

*Repositioning current product/service offerings:* When sales are going well and the economy is booming, many companies put off looking for new applications for current or planned offerings. Down times often persuade firms to look at alternative uses for product and service offerings.

At the same time, funding of these efforts is in short supply.

Nonetheless, they offer a growth alternative that many should consider.

A focus group participant detailed how his firm, which provided home loan services to banks and other financial institutions, discovered an alternative use for its database of home owners. It offered to generate leads for contractors and swimming pool installers. "It was tough for us to swing from servicing large institutions to working with smaller entities but we did it and are starting to recoup some of the revenues we lost when banks stopped making home loans," he said.

*Focusing on sales:* At all times, sales are a key ingredient in growth. In a down economy, it is often spoken of more than implemented in actuality, according to our respondents.

One long-time business owner said he hears colleagues preaching sales focus but often one of the first areas cut is the sales force. "Management looks at the sales force, sees them making big bucks and thinks that is the place to conserve resources," he said. "Actually, it is the one place that shouldn't be cut." Reinforcing this comment were the survey results in which 41% of respondents said they had cut one or more sales members in 2008.

What companies should be doing is pointing the sales force at achievable targets, preferably those clients who could best utilize their product/service offerings.

This focus group participant put his sales team in with the customer service group and gave them a goal of converting 25% of existing sales prospects. "You know," he said, "it's working. Six months into the program, and we are converting 45% of our prospects versus last year's 35%."

*Creating new products:* Another area that is often cut during down times is product development. Major corporations and smaller enterprises focus on current needs, often at the expense of long-term growth.

In our focus groups, many veteran participants said that was the worst decision they made in prior down cycles. One manager of a Utah software firm said, "Our venture backers made us cut product development to the bone in the last recession and it nearly cost us our position in the industry."

Other managers argued that new products were the lifeblood of any company and curtailing their development is putting a mortgage on the future.

All cautioned however, that funding these efforts should not be done if the company's survival is at stake. "For most firms, getting a new product to market means sapping resources and management has a difficult decision to make," said one participant. "But not moving ahead with promising offerings can often be counter-productive. Management should consider worker morale in making this decision. Employees stay at firms for perceived opportunities and if growth is somehow stopped, or perceived as being slowed, morale suffers."

*Restructuring marketing efforts:* While many of these recent points involve marketing, one of the major benefits to a challenging situation is that it encourages creative thinking. Marketing in down times often benefits from rethinking of priorities and emphasis.

Fully 71% of survey respondents said they had cut marketing expenses for 2009. This means their companies will need to do more with less.

Several respondents and group participants said that they instituted total reviews of their marketing efforts. Economies were found in their direct mail, promotion, advertising and customer response kits.

One participant said her firm had eliminated print material except for highly qualified prospects. This brought immediate rebuke from other participants who said printed materials were an absolute necessity, even in this age of the Internet. "There are places to cut and there are places you can't cut, and this is one of them," responded a Midwestern mechanical services company.

Another participant said his firm had identified 13% in postal and other mailing costs just by cleaning up their mailing list. "We were surprised at how much dead wood was on our lists," he said. In terms of promotion, one participant said, we went from four-color brochures to two-color and our budget for 2009 will be down 15% but our promotional schedule will not be cut."

Another area up for discussion was advertising. There was strong disagreement among participants as to where advertising should be cut. A majority of veteran managers said they stuck with their trade publications because they discovered they still generated the most cost effective leads.

Almost unanimously, participants and survey respondents said their firms were better positioned marketing-wise after they had re-engineered marketing in the face of adverse conditions.

## Strategy 6

*Talk more with your current client base and learn what their needs are.*

This strategy is suggested by Chris Stiehl, author of *Pain Killer Marketing*, a teacher at UC San Diego, and consultant to Fortune 500 companies. Have a brief but direct conversation with the business leader (CEO? Manager?) of each of your major customers, asking them what their major headaches are, how they could benefit from having those headaches solved, and how much it would mean to them – financially and in terms of peace of mind.

This approach is an excellent selling tool as well but should be viewed primarily as a fact-gathering mission. Ask for the time (about a half hour). If possible, make the meeting face-to-face. Don't do a survey, just ask about three or four basic questions. Tell them that you view them as a strategic partner and you would like to discover ways you could help each other. Learn how to listen.

Stiehl offers this real-life example of a client's confusion over the mediocre survey scores he was getting and the lack of understanding that he had of his customer service problems. He met with three of his CEO counterparts (three client companies) and had the brief heart-to-heart with them over individual meetings. As a result, the client discovered a service offering that eliminated one of the major problems of his clients, not only with his business but within their operations as well. He not only revived his company's relationship with the three customers, but found a new revenue stream. The key was to have the open conversation about how both parties could help each other.

## Strategy 7

*Closely manage accounts receivable, inventory and accounts payable.*

Keeping adequate cash on hand is one of the key strategies to stay in business. It is also a tool for growing the business because it forces you to look more closely at which clients are most profitable while also reviewing costs and where resources are placed.

Summit Resources' Brian Kinahan has 20+ years experience helping companies survive and thrive in difficult environments. He strongly suggests that companies review their accounts receivable aging report. Keep in mind that the collectability of a receivable decreases at a geometric rate the older it gets. Anything over 90 days is highly suspect. Some receivables may require the help of a collection agency but you can minimize that by using good practices within your own company. Here's how: Have someone with good interpersonal skills get on the phone and start calling customers who owe your company money. Be friendly, understanding, polite and firm; don't get off the phone without a commitment for immediate full payment or for a series of payments at specific dates. Place a friendly follow-up call on the scheduled payment date(s) to make sure everything is in order.

Calling serves many purposes. It makes you the squeaky wheel, it prevents operational snafus like "missing" invoices, and it builds relationships.

Once you get into the habit of doing this, and your customers understand that it's how you do business, then keep it going even in good times. It's simply good housekeeping. It will keep your accounts receivable current and small, and in turn boost liquidity and profits.

When sales slow, inventory days-on-hand grows. Go through your inventory categories or SKUs and determine how many months you have of each. Return whatever excess you can to your vendors in exchange for a refund or a credit to your account. Consider selling off any remaining inventory. Other companies might use the same raw materials and be interested in balancing out their inventories. Or there may be liquidators who will pay cents on the dollar for inventory that is of little real value to you. There's no point in holding on to it in hopes that it will be worth more later. In fact, every day your inventory sits on the shelf it's costing you money and declining in value. Keep this in mind as you consider alternatives, especially in deflationary times like these.

Pay your accounts payable as slowly as you can. You don't want to take advantage of your vendors and ruin a good relationship, but you can still slow things down. If you've been paying in 45 days you can try to move your payments out to 60 days or more. You'll want to communicate with your vendors so that they don't become alarmed and put you on COD or worse. Explain to them how you simply need to stretch out payments for a few extra days or weeks and try to get them to agree. If necessary you can offer to pay a small fee for the extra time. It might be worth it if they give you access to cash that your bank may not be making available.

One of the best ways of managing this process is to use an Intuit Workbook product to keep tabs of all expenses.

Utilizing this approach, one Canton, Missouri company was able to reduce postage and packaging costs by 33%, once they identified this area as having grown 55% in just two years while sales were up on 24%.

## Strategy 8

*Strive to put more value into product/service offerings before cutting prices.*

During down times, many search for products and services that are not only cheaper but offer more value. While pricing is important, value will often tip the balance in a sales shoot-out.

Many companies switch to a "lower-price" strategy. Many retailers are trumpeting price reductions as a key to sales. They are still reporting sales declines. However, Wal-Mart, with its emphasis on value, has maintained and even grown sales during this time of economic upheaval.

By emphasizing the value-proposition companies will be able to maintain profit margins.

One focus group participant reported that his service company switched to emphasizing the quality of their offerings during the previous downturn and was able to add clients while competitors were losing customers.

A New Jersey cleaning company, faced with a reduction in cleaning schedules by three major banking clients offered to include document shredding in branches at no additional cost. This met with positive response from the clients and they were able to head off the schedule reduction.

## Strategy 9

*Stick with what the company knows best and don't be too quick to jump.*

There is a temptation in times of stress to look for alternative opportunities outside the main business model. This can take the form of moving into new sectors; adding products that are not complementary to the main offerings; or acquiring new resources because they are attractively priced.

In the focus groups, veteran managers talked about some of the alternatives they looked at during prior down times. Most said they had resisted the temptation to move into areas which were far away from their main business line. Laughed another, "sometimes the best deals are the ones you don't make and when I think of the things we looked at, I shudder."

All participants said that they did introduce new products or services but only if they had been in planning before the downturn or made sense given what their main businesses were.

Survey respondents said they were focusing on strengthening their current business offerings and not moving forward with radical departures from them.

During the dot com bust early in this decade, a company that delivered groceries through an online portal found it was losing money delivering drug items in addition to their core items. It made the tough decision to discontinue this part of the business and was able to survive through the down period and thrive as times got better.

## Strategy 10

*Be proactive and position the company for growth now and in the future.*

Above all, remain proactive in meeting the challenges of these times. Most of your clients and suppliers are in the same boat. Create solutions to problems as they are presented and share them openly with staff so that they are team efforts. Share those solutions with clients and suppliers and make them part of the resolution. Growing in times of stress is based more on perception than actuality as others are more likely looking for help and guidance. Those with a plan and a will to implement can become leaders. By being a leader, growth is made easier and more profitable. Don't hang back, if an opportunity presents itself, take it. Remain positive and upbeat and don't, under any circumstances reveal doubts or fears to anyone outside your immediate confidants.

Throughout the focus groups, manager after manager repeated the mantra of positive outlook being the key to successfully surviving and more importantly, growing.

This approach was summed up by a veteran who likened a downturn to a strategic retreat. "It's how you position your resources and stay poised to take advantage of any opportunities that present themselves. The really courageous ones will grow their companies in this time of trouble."

As one company owner reported, she kept up a positive front through the entire period and when better times appeared, many customers told her that this approach convinced them she would survive. This encouraged them to continue patronizing her business when they were cutting back on other vendors.

# GLOSSARY

**2.0:**   Web 2.0 refers to a perceived second generation of web development and design that facilitates communication, secure information sharing, interoperability, and collaboration on the World Wide Web.

**B2B:**   Business to business; describes commerce transactions between businesses, such as between a manufacturer and a wholesaler, or between a wholesaler and a retailer.

**Blogs:**   A type of "citizen's journalism." The term, a contraction of the term weblog, is a type of website, usually maintained by an individual with regular entries of commentary, descriptions of events, or other material such as graphics or video.

**Broadcast:**   Distribution of audio and/or video signals which transmit programs to an audience; includes radio, TV, cable and telephone.

**Conversion:**   In marketing, a conversion occurs when a prospective customer takes the marketer's intended action. If the prospect has visited a marketer's web site, the conversion action might be making an online purchase, or submitting a form to request additional information. The conversion rate is the percentage of visitors who take the conversion action.

**Direct mail:**     This involves commercial communication, usually unsolicited. It is focused on driving purchases that can be attributed to a specific "call-to-action."

**Index or home page:**   The front page or main page of a website.

**Janus Principle:**       A process that centers on understanding the marketplace and the organization's own internal prejudices.  It enables the marketer to proceed on the basis of not what the organization wants or expects but rather what can be done to meet the marketplace's needs.

**Landing page:**   In online marketing a landing page, sometimes known as a lead capture page, is the page that appears when a potential customer clicks on an advertisement or a search-engine result link.

**List:**   A group of email addresses of people that are interested in the same subject; includes affiliation, response and complied lists.

**Microsites:**     Page groups of personalized content. Also known as a mini-site or weblet is an individual web page(s) which are meant to function as an auxiliary supplement to a primary website.

**MMA:**    Mobile Marketing Association is an international non-profit industry trade group that represents over 600 agencies, advertisers, hand-held device manufacturers, wireless operators, aggregators, technology enablers, market research firms and other companies focused on marketing via the mobile channel.

**One-to-one marketing:**    Personalized marketing is an extreme form of product differentiation. Whereas product differentiation tries to differentiate a product from competing ones, personalization tries to make a unique product offering for each customer.

**Online:**     Indicates a state of connectivity; includes websites, emails, micro-sites, blogs, texting, wikis, webcasts, pod casts, etc.

**Open rate:**   The email open rate is a measure primarily used by marketers as an indication of how many people "view" or "open" the commercial electronic mail they send out.

**Out-of-office:**    Essentially any type of advertising that reaches the business person (consumer) while he or she is outside the office; channels include transportation vehicles, transit points, hotels, restaurants, etc.

**PR:**    Public relations; the practice of managing the flow of information between an organization and its publics. PR gains an organization or individual exposure to their audiences using topics of public interest and news items that do not require direct payment.

**Paid advertising:**    Communication that typically attempts to persuade potential customers to purchase or to consume more of a particular brand of product or service.

**Podcasts:**    A series of digital media files, usually digital audio or video that is made available for download via Web syndication.

**Print:**    Reproduced text and images, typically with ink on paper; includes trade press, national media, newspapers, books.

**ROI:**    Return on investment; the ratio of money gained or lost (realized or unrealized) on an investment relative to the amount of money invested.

**RSS Feeds:**    Really Simple Syndication is a family of Web feed formats used to publish frequently updated works – such as blog entries, news headlines, audio, and video – in a standardized format.

**SEO:**    Search Engine Optimization; the process of improving the volume and quality of traffic to a web site from search engines via "natural" ("organic" or "algorithmic") search results.

**SME:**    Small and medium enterprises (also small and medium businesses: SMBs); companies whose headcount or turnover falls below certain limits.

**Social networks:**      A social structure made of nodes (which are generally individuals or organizations) that are tied by one or more specific types of interdependency, such as values, visions, ideas, financial exchange, friendship, sexual relationships, kinship, dislike, conflict or trade.

**Spam:**    The abuse of electronic messaging systems (including most broadcast mediums, digital delivery systems) to send unsolicited bulk messages indiscriminately. While the most widely recognized form of spam is e-mail spam, which involves nearly identical messages sent to numerous recipients by e-mail.

**Trade press:**     A periodical, magazine or publication printed with the intention of target marketing to a specific industry or type of trade/business.

**Transpromotion:**     Exchange promotion with non-competitors, e.g., inserts in statements. Transpromotional documents combine CRM Customer relationship management and data mining technology with Variable data printing and location intelligence. This powerful combination reduces the cost of traditional statement printing by sharing the print spend with a marketing spend while reaching the prospect base of all existing customers.

**VAR:**    Value Added Reseller is a company that adds some feature(s) to an existing product(s), and then resells it (usually to end-users) as an integrated product or complete "turn-key" solution.

**Viral marketing:**     Marketing techniques that use pre-existing social networks to produce increases in brand awareness or to achieve other marketing objectives (such as product sales) through self-replicating viral processes. Creates web content that readers want to read or consume and share with others; Spreads ideas or information.

**VoIP:**     Voice over Internet Protocol; a general term for a family of transmission technologies for delivery of voice communications over IP networks such as the Internet or other packet-switched networks.

**Web conferencing:**    Live meetings or presentations over the Internet.

**Webcasts:**    Media files distributed over the Internet using streaming media technology. A webcast may either be distributed live or on demand. Essentially, webcasting is "broadcasting" over the Internet.

**Webinars:**   A one-way web conference from the speaker to the audience with limited audience interaction, such as in a webcast. Often collaborative, including polling or Q & A sessions.

**White Paper:**    An authoritative report or guide that often addresses problems and how to solve them. White Papers are used to educate readers and help people make decisions.

**Wikis:**    A collection of Web pages designed to enable anyone with access to contribute or modify content, using a simplified markup language.

# INDEX

Brick Tower Press
New York

For sales, editorial information, subsidiary rights information
or a catalog, please write, phone or e-mail:

Brick Tower Press
1230 Park Avenue
New York, New York 10128, US
Sales: 1-800-68-BRICK
Tel: 212-427-7139 • Fax: 212-860-8852
www.BrickTowerPress.com
email: bricktower@aol.com


For sales in the United States, please contact:

National Book Network
nbnbooks.com
Orders: 800-462-6420
Fax: 800-338-4550
email: custserv@nbnbooks.com


For sales in the UK and Europe, please contact:

Gazelle Book Services
Falcon House, Queens Square
Lancaster, LA1 1RN, UK
Tel: (01524) 68765 • Fax: (01524) 63232
email: gazelle4go@aol.com


For sales in Australia and New Zealand, please contact:

Bookwise International
174 Cormack Road,Wingfield, 5013, South Australia
Tel: 61 (0) 419 340056 • Fax: 61 (0) 8 8268 1010
email: karen.emmerson@bookwise.com.au